Pause for thought

When taking the first step on your journey towards your goals, keep in mind the following quote, it will keep you focused and safe whilst on your journey:

"The strength of the team is the leader; the strength of the leader is the team"

(Leading for Success)

"Taking the First Step"

"A journey towards your Goals"

David Keough

© 2018 David Keough, Publisher,
Leading for Success,
3 Station Court,
Harrogate,
North Yorkshire,
UK
HG3 1BF

Taking the First Step

Content

- Dedication
- Introduction
- Workplace Perspectives
- Step One –   Self Awareness
- Step Two –   Transition (Planning)
- Step Three -   Communication
- Step Four –   Personality Traits
- Step Five -   Leader v Manager
- Summary
- About the Author
- Resource Guide

Dedication

"Taking the first step" is dedicated to my family who never lost their belief that one day I would succeed. Especially during those long lonely times, staring defeat in the face, were darkness appears to be your only friend, and when others can only offer encouragement for you to give up on your dream.

To Martin and Claire, for their creative art work and illustrations contained in this book.

Finally to you, the brave men and women, who get up every day to try again, not knowing if today could be the day; that you finally achieve your vision, or like yesterday, you have to pick yourself up, dust yourself down, and go again. Never giving up and continually taking small steps forward to success; burning the bridges behind you that you have just crossed, so there is no turning back on your dream. It is not how many times you fall down; it is how many times you get up again. Be strong and do not stop believing in you and the process in this book.

When I refer to "I" in "Taking the First Step", I refer to you the reader. The reason for this is that you the reader are psychologically instilling the process and changes in yourself as you go through the book, that are needed to deliver on your goals and ultimately achieve it. It keeps you in a frame of mind that you have achieved it and the potential pitfalls that you have overcome to get there. It gets you to believe that you can achieve and you can be successful.

Obviously I have gone through the process and learning's to be able to help you deliver on your goals and achieve what you may think as impossible, become possible.

Finally to the people who had written me off, as "aiming to high" they said," it can't be done" they said, " get your head out of the clouds" they said .To the people who didn't believe I could do it, to the judgemental who thought my dreams were just pie in the sky. Please note "They are your limitations, not mine".

Hopefully after you have read this book, you will want to change your perspective and achieve your dreams, by believing in you and others, removing those self-limitations that are holding you back. You too can do it; you can take that first step and go beyond; just believe the impossible is always possible and not only follow the process before you; own it- OWN THE PROCESS.

THE MAN IN THE ARENA

It is not the critic who counts; not the man who points out how the strong man stumbles,

or where the doer of deeds could have done them better.

The credit belongs to the man who is actually in the arena,

Whose face is marred by dust and sweat and blood;

who strives valiantly; who errs, who comes short again and again,

because there is no effort without error and shortcoming;

but who does actually strive to do the deeds;

who knows great enthusiasms, the great devotions;

who spends himself in a worthy cause;

who at the best knows in the end the triumph of high achievement,

and who at the worst, if he fails, at least fails while daring greatly,

so that his place shall never be with those cold and timid souls ,

who neither know victory nor defeat.

Theodore Roosevelt (23/04/1910)

Introduction

As a leader, how many times have I asked myself the question, "What do I need to do, to get my staff motivated for me to achieve my vision?"

I have tried everything, sending the staff out on course after course, getting in motivational speakers, incentivising them, cajoling them, recommending every self-help book on the shelf and dare I say it, even threatened them.

How many times after a meeting, seminar or training session, the staff, are all fired up as they leave the room and by the time they have reached the car park or are back at their desk, they have reverted back to type, lost the enthusiasm and think, what's the use, it won't work anyway?

Putting every person through the same car wash of training and hoping they come out the other side with a new clean, shiny attitude and behavioural change, is wishful thinking. It simply does not work. Traditional training is only 10-20% effective at best; not a brilliant return on my investment and their development.

For me to be a great leader, I have to have people who want to learn, develop and be led; most importantly, led by me; The Boss, the one they look to for inspiration, motivation and a vision to include all; who is committed to the vision and to them, fulfilling my role in the collective team and delivering my part of achieving my goals.

So why isn't it working? Why am I not seeing the changes I need to be an effective leader?

Here is a possible reason why!

Am I trying to change behaviours by opinions rather than positive actions? Am I leading by example, only operating from a positive frame of mind and out front doing the trailblazing? Using opinions only to change behaviour is counterproductive and only leads to confusion, resentment.

If business had an external assessor and the same stringent rules that Health and Safety carries, for employee relations and management style; I would imagine quite a few would be closed down or given notice, for creating an unsafe and toxic environment to work in, until the recommendations have been implemented. This type of working environment is archaic and has no place in modern working practices; times have changed, we have to change and adapt to be successful.

Any change in a person's behaviour has to take place at a deeper level; permanent change will only take place in the unconscious mind where traditional training does not fully reach, to have the impact on those behavioural changes I desire.

Values are the key to unlocking the mind and allow change to take place; values sit nestled in the unconscious mind calling the shots for us. Values either motivate us to do something or demotivate us not to do something. Values drive our behaviours, they underpin our attitude and personality, values form our views on life-they are our key decision filters. Values sit in the unconscious mind and everything we do stem from them, values will always operate in a positive way for us. The unconscious mind is there to protect us, always; and values have a positive intention with everything we do or don't do. If I need change to take place, I need to operate with the values system, because that is what, is important to people.

When drawing up my company values, it is far more important than putting a few nice ideas or statements on a piece of paper or a website to say we have some. My company has to stand or fall by them; they have to be meaningful, purposeful and be genuinely lived by-by all in the business.

Take a moment to examine your own and your company's values now, ask the following questions:
- Who thought up the values?
- What is the thinking behind the values?
- Are the values still appropriate for my business?
- Are the values achieving what they were meant to achieve?
- How do the values sit with my business plan? - After all they go hand in hand.
- Does every one understand and use them? If not why not.
- Does your business operate always using the values?

Take for example: three friends go to the cinema together, they watch the same movie at the same time, they sit next to each other, and they share the same experience. Yet ask each of them after the movie " What did they enjoy most about the movie" you will more often than not have three different answers and you are left scratching your head wondering if they did watch the same movie. Same scenario in your meetings or training, everyone will take away different things that are important to them, that may not be important to others. These are people's values coming into play on how they perceive the situation. They decided according to what is important to them and what is not through their value system, their life experiences and how those experiences are interpreted. Are your business meetings productive and effective? If not, I would suggest looking at the company values and see if the meetings are being delivered with the values underpinning it.

A classic you always hear is, "I'm a different person out of work, I behave completely the opposite to when I'm sitting behind my desk" You cannot be two different people-

Impossible, you just have a different set of values for a different situation that adapts your behaviour to suit.

So as I have established, values drive our behaviours, so I have to change our values to get the results I desire; a change in behaviour. Have you ever tried to change someone's behaviour, easier said than done? It is far easier to change a value, and it becomes a permanent change rather than a short term gain.

For me to achieve this, as I now know, all of our individual values are different. I need to establish a set of values and behaviours that are acceptable, meaningful and underpin the culture of the work place that the entire workforce adheres to. Values will give people strength and power, if abused; it will render the person weak and powerless. Values once installed need to be lived and breathed by everyone in the business and led from the top-by me.

My culture will be formed from our values, as culture is a combination of values and my goals delivered by my language and behaviours.

Values need to be enforced once set, with iron determination so I can function as a collective organisation and with every employee playing a vital, fully inclusive role in the business and the vision.

Creating a business that functions as one that brings your vision to life through collective excellence, has to be done through values. Understanding the importance of values and the impact they have on you and others is the critical factor in human behaviour. They either motivate us or demotivate us to do something.

Understanding values will help me understand me; and others, once I achieve this, the rest will fall into place, the pieces will start to fit together just like a jigsaw.

These values cannot just be yours and imposing them onto the staff. It does not work that way as we will explore later on in the book.

A value only has a value, when the value is valued; otherwise it just becomes a wish list, a shopping list of wanting, change by chance and not by choice. Waiting on chance to sort out your business, will only put your decision making into the hands of others, they will control the destination of you and your business. You as a leader will become defunct and irrelevant in your own business.

So take charge of the situation, make a positive impact for the future through change and control the direction and destination of your business.

"I now never underestimate or undervalue a value"

Leader of the Organisations Perspective

What is it like being at the top of the organisation when you feel that you are the only one who really cares about the business?

You seem to shoulder the entire burden, the responsibilities, being accountable to everyone and everything. Yes the buck stops with you, however, why isn't it being headed off at the pass before hand? That's what you're paying the staff for.

Well in reality that is probably true. Nobody else will care as much about the business as you; after all you have invested your hard earned cash into the business and have the greatest amount to lose. It is more difficult for you to walk away from the business when things are getting tough: unlike an employee, they can hop onto the bandwagon of another recruitment agency in the search for other riches elsewhere.

Getting buy in from the entire employee's is essential to giving you the best chance of succeeding and making your business a strong and healthy successful one.

You cannot do it alone or just rely on one or two loyal staff to get you to where you want to be. An all-inclusive, well informed and motivated workforce is the key to unlocking the full potential of your business. As you can gather, you cannot continue on this spiral of frustration, lack of commitment and being lonely at the top. It is not productive and certainly is not conducive to good health.

How do I achieve that?

How do I find the illusive formula that will get me what I want?

Manager of the Organisations Perspective

As a manager in the business and being responsible for teams of employees are you getting the best out of them through great leadership and inspiring development? Are you the driving force behind the business and bringing to life the vision of the boss, hitting and exceeding targets, generating new business and maximising existing business?

Or is it the opposite, are you operating in the pressure cooker environment? Getting pressured from the boss at the top to get results and get the team motivated. Getting pressured from the sides by suppliers and customers, and getting pressured from underneath by the staff demanding more of your time to sort out issues and not understanding what they are supposed to be doing. Most of your day is being spent on HR issues and fire fighting with never enough hours in the day to get your work done. Eating lunch at your desk as you keep on working through, not allowing yourself to take a break, as you slave away to meet the deadlines, taking work home and using all of your spare time catching up. Stress and burn out is slowly becoming your only friend who really understand what you are going through, as the boss demands more and the staffs creates more havoc.

Is it all worth it, stuck in a trap with nowhere to turn and not sure how to turn it around, is this what, management is about? "Surely it has to be better than this"

Later in the book I will help you unravel the mess, pick you up and put you back onto the path of success where you want to be and what you expected the job was about.

A manager's role now is so different and far tougher than 20 years ago. New workers' rights- which are forever being changed, with the digital age you are only a click away from work 24 hours a day, 7 days a week in any part of the world. Constant change at the click of a button, new demands being loaded onto your desk at an alarming speed. Don't be too hard on yourself; I can help you take control of the situation. I will show you what motivates and demotivates the work force, how to communicate, so the message is understood and how to get others being accountable and removing the endless HR issues that burden you every day. It is estimated that in today's modern working environment, managers spend 40% of their time on HR issues which is taking them away from their duties and putting unnecessary pressure on them causing stress and burnout. As a manager you're probably feeling that the boss is okay, as he doesn't have to deal with all these HR issues and the staff are ok as they don't have to deal with the pressure from the boss, and being the manager, the staff believe it's my job anyway to deal with all the flack.

As you read further on in the book, you will discover ways of breaking that cycle of the pressure cooker environment and break down barriers that are holding you back.

Staff of the Organisations Perspective

When signing your contract to be part of the business, we're you thinking; I am so happy to have been offered the job out of all the other candidates, great moving here, can forge a new career and can't wait to get started in your new role.

What a difference a few weeks makes, politics, back stabbing, lazy colleagues, high absenteeism and an unhealthy atmosphere hanging over the place. Are you wishing your days away watching the clock to home time? So you can escape the jungle and get back to some normality away from work.

The manager wants more from you, yet you don't know what he wants as he is so stressed out and only giving half cooked messages and instructions. Nobody else wants to help and all you hear is "Not my job better ask someone else", and what on earth are the company's values and vision I keep hearing being kicked about. I haven't seen either of them, do they even exist. Who is actually running the business, this place is out of control, no one in charge, no direction and certainly no togetherness from anyone.

Confusion, inconsistencies and a complete lack of direction is the daily routine in the business.

All these promises that were made to me at the interview, nowhere to be heard or seen, it certainly is the old mushroom syndrome down at the bottom- kept in the dark and fed manure all day! Well if I can't beat them, I may as well join them and do as little as possible and search for another job.

As a staff member, you probably feel that the boss and managers are ok, because they are not involved in these cliques and negativity that runs through the team, if that's what you can actually call them.

As you read further on in the book, you will discover how the company values and vision will become integral for all in the business, how they shape great organisations and become the business that people want to be a part of. Working in a company through collective excellence, where everyone in the business is part of the vision, no matter how small or big that contribution is. Being valued and respected and treated as an individual, with great leadership and development in place every step of the way.

As you can probably conclude from the different perspectives, we all want the same thing, yet all three have huge differences in expectations and a huge gulf in communication. Every level believes that the other levels are fine and having an easy ride on a daily basis and not having to deal with all the issues that you find yourself in.

It couldn't be further from the truth, each level is suffering because they are in the centre of the negative spiral and cannot see the wood for the trees.

The situation we find ourselves in here can only be resolved through collective change, by creating positive choices. The choices we can use to bring about the required changes are:
All three choices have to fit together; this underpins collective excellence in the business. I needed to communicate effectively my vision; everyone needed to understand exactly what I will achieve and how I will achieve it.

- Establish where the business is now.
- Where I want it to be.
- What I need to change to take it to where I want it to be.
- How will those changes work to achieve the desired results?
- How will I know when I have achieved it?

The Business has to have a clear Vision and the Vision has to be clearly communicated and understood by each person in the business.

> *No ambiguity, no misinterpretations or loose strands in order to put one's own meaning to the vision*

The Business has to have very clear and precise outcome settings. They need to know where they are and where they want to be, moving from what to what. The outcome has to be planned, communicated to every person in the business, so we all know what is required from us and the purpose for doing what we are doing.

> *No ambiguity, no misinterpretations or loose strands in order to put one's own meaning to the vision*

Setting agreed Values and Behaviours for the business that each person observes an carries them out without question to the letter

> *No ambiguity, no misinterpretations or loose strands in order to put one's own meaning to the vision*

Vision in Action: Executing Strategy through Behavioural Change

Getting my goals into action; the purpose is the delivery of a collective excellence culture in the work place for the common goal

Step 1: Awareness
The first step is to establish awareness of the organisation's current delivery of excellence culture. Everyone gets clarity over the business' true purpose and what they're doing to achieve it, by understanding themselves, each other and a way of thinking which puts them in tune with the vision

How it's done:

I have the individuals/team to step back and take an outsider's view of their behaviours, habits, strengths and weakness. This is a completely honest, non-judgemental safe environment so they can experience the impact they have on themselves, each other and the business. This is not about hitting people with a stick or belittling each other, but to enable the team to bond and to share ideas, experience and best practice. Through this, it creates a true supportive network to allow people to deliver on your goals.

The significance of part 1 is to get the individuals tuned into them, tuned into the team and crucially aligned and tuned to my goals and deliver on my business objects.

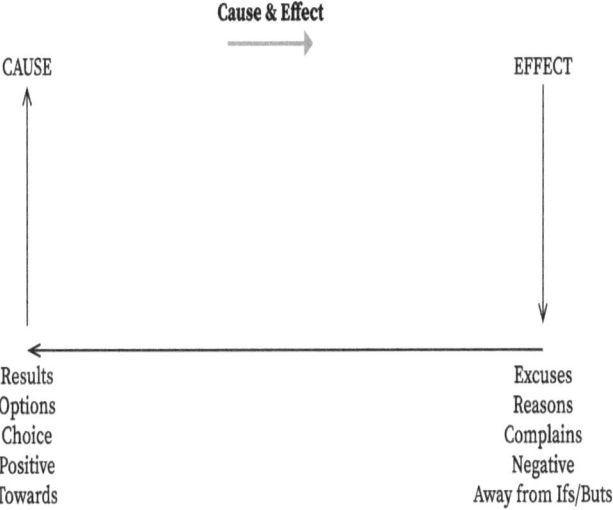

To be in control of everything I did to achieve my goals, I had to be at cause at all times, along with my teams. We had to take responsibility and accountability for everything that happened in our business, and not leaving ourselves exposed to chance and dancing to other people's tunes to compromise on my goals. Being constantly at cause kept us focused, in a positive frame of mind and without excuses to compromise or water down my vision.

Once the teams understood this model, they took responsibility and accountability for everything that they did; they all started to grow, develop and their thinking became more as a leaders would think. Clock watching, gossiping and negativity were collapsing before our eyes, as there was no place for it, it did not belong anymore in my business.

The Cause and Effect model is very simple, yet crucial to achievement in anything you wish to do. Its gives people empowerment and autonomy used in great leadership qualities, which builds and enhances everyone else they come into contact with. It builds character and is fundamental to people relationships in the workplace through honesty, trust, respect and dignity. It keeps my behaviour appropriate at all times and stops the blame game or passing the buck when things go wrong.

Reversing of the cause and effect model, to highlight issues

One of the first things I did when using cause and effect, was to reverse it around- putting effect first and then cause.

This I found was very good in pinpointing the results /effects that I was getting, and then I could focus on what was causing them. It became for me an important analytical tool to see where change in my behaviours needed to take place in order for me to achieve my goals.

Only by doing this could I plan effectively and put everything else into place on the foundation to build my vision. Cause and effect is in a nutshell, consequences from my actions. If the results are not what I want, what is causing them? What am I not doing right? What is causing me to have these consequences?

The Conscious Mind V the Unconscious Mind

The unconscious mind is there to protect me at all times, that is its primary function. It acts like a data base, the hard drive that stores and retains all of my experiences, values, beliefs, habits, emotions and long term memories.
The conscious mind is more like the software; it is rational, logical, and analytical, holds my short term memories and it contains my will power. All of my goals, visions are conceived in the conscious mind, however, whether I achieve them or not, is governed by my unconscious mind.

The unconscious mind is approximately 9/10s of the decision making process. This reason alone is why it is difficult to achieve goals and keep New Year resolutions; the unconscious mind is set in its ways, programmed over years of information and experiences that have now been firmly established as my habits and values. It will mostly overrule the conscious mind, and fight against any change. The unconscious mind controls me, it determines what I will or will not do what I can achieve and what I cannot, it is my driving force.

Something's we need to understand about the unconscious mind that makes it powerful are;

- It stores and retains all the information that it is given
- It stores every experiences and the information it is given
- There are no fuzzy areas, everything is black and white
- It cannot deal with negativity, everything that enters it, is formed into a positive experience. Even those little voice of negativity inside it are turned into a positive

- voice as it protects me from doing something that may make me look silly or fail to succeed
- It controls my habits
- Its primary task is to protect me

Because the unconscious minds primary task is there to protect me, any change has to be beneficial to me for it to accept it. The conscious mind has the ability to be rational or critical of new suggestions or to compare possible actions. The unconscious mind will use its power to protect me by using its best action to ensure it deals with the situation in the quickest possible way.

Understanding this principle, now makes me understand that all permanent change has to be done in the unconscious mind. In order to do this, I need to change my values so they can be aligned with my vision. Values either motivate me to do something or demotivate me not to do something.

If I need to change my team's perspective to achieve my vision, I have to operate with a value based process. It has to have a value to them; it has to carry an importance as to why they are doing it. This value isn't about monetary, this is about their individual identity, and will their unconscious mind allow this change to happen.

The way I approached this was to set collective values in the business, values that we all contributed to and discussed.

With the teams, we came up with 5 top values, core values of how the business would operate. To go with each value, we had to determine, what behaviours go with each value, this was important, as I know that if the value is the driver behind the behaviour, so that is what I needed to do.

The very positive thing about collective values is they become self-governing and create a culture that has been created by all and not just me imposing my values on them. By imposing my values on them is meaningless, they are not important to them, it disengages them and they do not buy into my vision

CONSCIOUS AND UNCONSCIOUS MINDS

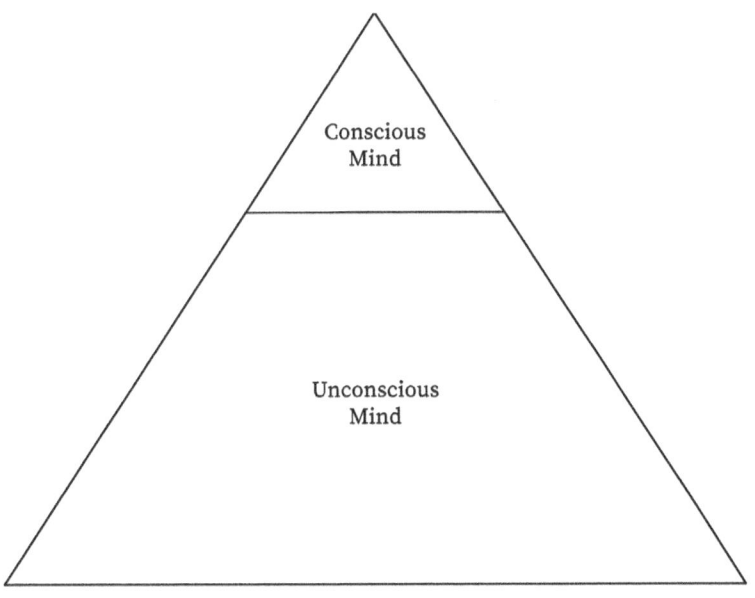

The unconscious mind makes up the vast proportion of the both minds; the unconscious mind is likened to the hard drive of a computer and the conscious mind the software element

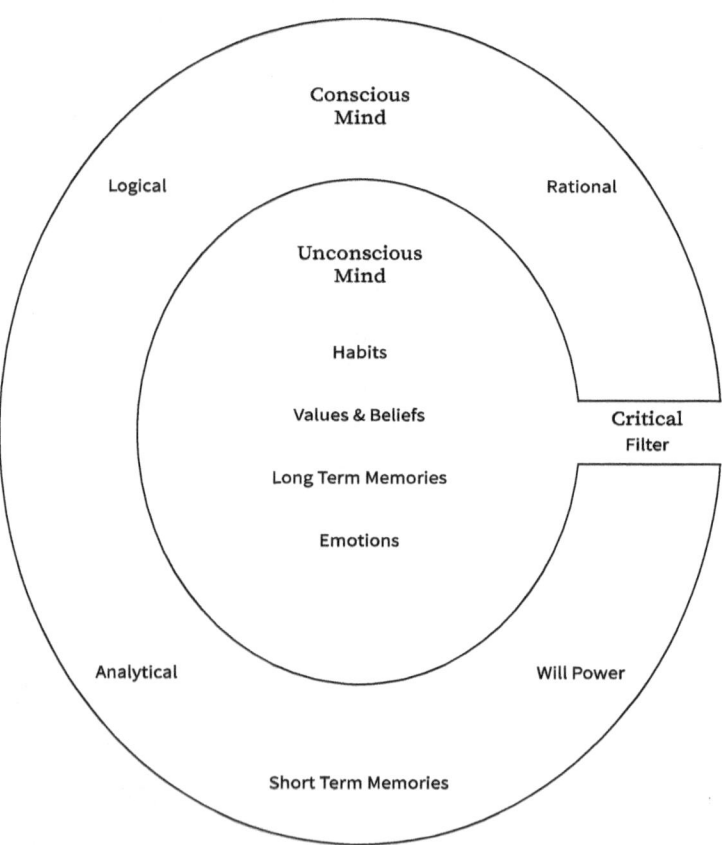

Personality

"My actions are an external display of my internal state"

Every day I make judgements about people by using their personality as a measured guide about them.

This judgement will determine whether I like a person or whether I do not like a person. Whether I employ that person, whether I promote that person – generally I build or create a world around that person of what I believe that person is or isn't, based solely on my experiences and how I interpret and project those experiences onto that person.

I talk about personality as an everyday word or subject, however-do I understand what personality really is?

What is personality and how is it formed?

Values + Beliefs = Our Attitude which is Driving our Behaviour.

Add in our Memories and Experiences, how we understand them, that then gives us our personality.

Values + Beliefs = Our Attitude which is Driving our Behaviour.
+
Our Memories & Experiences

=
OUR PERSONALITY

This highlights the importance of values, the underlying power of them and why when dealing with my teams, planning, meetings; they have to come into play as they underpin everything and everyone.

Values will determine if I will succeed or not. They make up the backbone that supports all HR, Operations, ER, Planning, long and short term objectives, Rewards-my whole business, everything hangs off my company values.

Never undervalue a value, the consequences are not worth it; it leaves you treading water in a state of frustration.

Values and Beliefs

What are values? Why are they important?

Values are exactly what it means, something which is very valuable or important to us and forms part of our makeup, our identity. When challenging some ones values or beliefs, do so with great care and respect as you start to challenge a person's identity, their sole existence and how they live their lives. Try another person's value or belief on for size to see how it fits; only then will you start to get an understanding of what it means to others.

To influence change in others, I had to work with peoples values and match them up to my vision, create a set of shared values and behaviours for the business for us all to work for one common goal.

Values exert a powerful effect upon our life. They determine how you relate to your family and you're partner, what products you buy, how you perform your job and whom you vote for. Values dictate your leisure time activities, your interests, what you learn, and your religious convictions and so on. The 'generation gap' is a statement about values.

Toward values will drive you towards pleasure, were away values would drive you away from pain. Away values are generally indicative of negative emotions or negative decisions, focusing on what we don't have and what we don't want. Towards values would be the reverse or opposite of the negative values, focusing on what we have and what we want

Values are our unconscious minds motivators and de-motivators, they affect our choices. Values are important, as they are the motivators that drive our behaviours; it is because of our values that we do something, what's important to us or what is not important. Once we have done something, we use our values to judge whether what we have done is either good or bad from our own perspective.

Beliefs

"Beliefs tend to fulfil themselves".

What are beliefs? Why are they important?

Beliefs are closely held generalisations and assumptions we make about ourselves, about others in the world and about how we expect things to be. Emotionally held options treated as facts and the basis of our everyday decisions, skills and behaviours.

They are important because they form the basis of our reality, our view and interpretation of the world.

Our values are things that we deem important and can include concepts like – equality, honesty, education, effort, perseverance, loyalty, faithfulness, conservation of the environment and many other concepts.

Beliefs are basically assumptions that we make about the world and our values stem from those beliefs. Our beliefs grow from what we see, hear, experience, read and think about. From these things we develop an opinion that we hold to be true and unmovable at that time. From our beliefs we derive our values, which can either be correct or incorrect when compared with evidence, but nonetheless hold true for us.

1. Beliefs- are concepts that we hold to be true.
2. Values- are ideas that we hold to be important.
3. Values- govern the way we behave, communicate and interact with others
4. Beliefs- govern our thoughts
5. Beliefs- and values determine our attitudes and opinions.

The powerful part of our being is our belief system, which decides our personality and what we become physically and mentally. What we perceive and accept forms our belief system. Our subconscious mind accepts what we perceive whether it is true or false, positive or negative and drops it in to our belief system which later becomes reality.

Once we entered the world we are in a blank state, we have no ideas about the world and how it works. Human beings were genetically programmed to model or mimic those around them, because of that we are easily influenced by external influences.

Our first influence comes from our Parents then our relatives and friends. We learn most of the things from our parents what we can or cannot do, most children sooner or later adopt their parents belief system which in turn limits them and filters their reality.

Core beliefs are fundamental judgements that will influence all of our other experiences followed on behind them. They are generally related to perceptions about identity and as such they have become a focal point around which our other beliefs about others, our environment and us are formed and organised. If we believe that the world is a dark, nasty unfriendly place, then our beliefs, ideas and perceptions will be influenced and formed around our basic core belief. The core beliefs are usually and importantly self-fulfilling.

> **"Whether you believe you can, or whether you believe you can't- you are right"**
> **Henry Ford**

Blind Spots

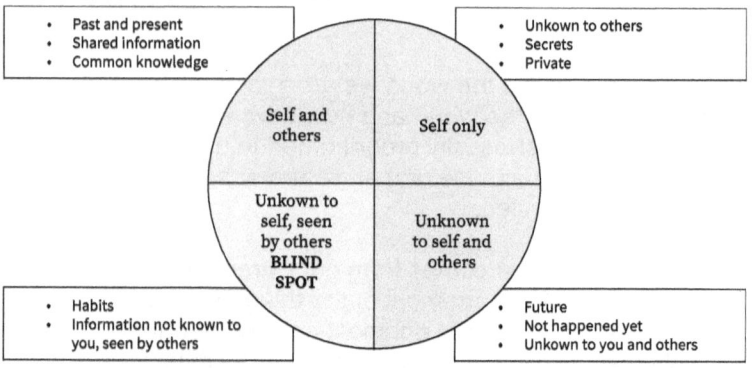

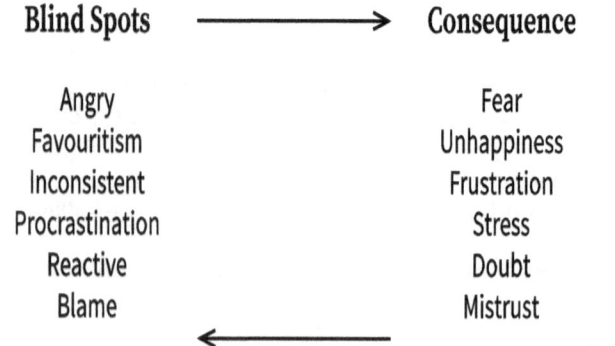

Just the same as cause and effect; there are consequences to my actions, those consequences can have a detrimental effect on my business if I am not aware of my actions and responses. Blind spots are crucial in understanding my own behaviours and having self-awareness in everything I do, remember- i cannot, not communicate.

Blind spots make me see things from a one dimensional perspective, my own take on things without the consideration of others. Not a healthy situation to be firmly entrenched in and consistently making decisions from. It becomes a dictatorship style of running a business. It creates for me a closed mind; not open to suggestions or change, leading to an environment that has a culture of mistrust and everyone else is wrong.

Not being aware of what I say or how I react to certain situations can have a devastating impact on moral and relationships in the workplace. Blind spots are formed from habits that at one time would have been useful to me, however now they are not appropriate to use today, as I have grown and developed they have become out-dated. Because they are my old habits, they have now become my natural reactions to certain situations or events-hence the saying "I can read you like an open book" or "I knew you would behave like this if I told you".

Blind spots can become very dangerous as others will not open up to me, raise concerns or issues, instead they will bury them underground where the gossip mill churns away. They will expose my weaknesses or chinks in my armour so others know how to play me and get what they wish. They could compromise my vision by playing on those imperfections, and play one another off against each other.

People watch everything I do, listen to everything I say and remember those feelings, stored away in a place in the unconscious mind- ready to use against me when the time suited them.

The teams knew more about me than I knew about me, things I have never told them or discussed with them. They knew it from my blind spots and would try to use it to suit them for their own ends

Being self-aware is essential as a leader, it helped me understand myself, and only then, could I begin to try and understand others. I want to respond to situations and not just react, a measured response and thought process given appropriately to the situation at hand; not just a knee jerk reaction which gives possible short term solutions, however it creates long term headaches.

My new Understandings

These were my new understandings, what were yours and how did you apply them?

Highly motivated individuals and teams achieve the common goal by understanding each other and themselves. Only by understanding ourselves do we have any realistic chance of understanding others.

The greatest gift I could give my teams was my time. The time to listen to them irrespective of how busy I was or how much I rather have not have to sit there. Giving the teams quality time to listen, opened up lines of communication that once where thought impossible.

It builds team spirit, honesty, trust, respect and I got to know my teams on a more individual basis and a personal level by taking interest in them. I became very aware of them, aware of what has happening around me and my own self-awareness.

Leaving talking to the teams for the once a year appraisal or performance review, was now removed from my business. It was ineffective and a tick box exercise to say it had be done and in some cases, bury bad news.

Values underpin me, my individual people in the teams and the culture in the work place. I need to nurture them, protect them and be mindful of them at all times.

- *A value only has a value if the value is being valued.*
- *A person only has a value if the person is being valued*
- *My vision only has a value if the vision is being valued*

Values really are the spine of a business and an individual- I have learned to never underestimate or undervalue a value in anything or anyone.

Step 2: Transition

The second step I got a very clear understanding on where the business is now, where I want it to be "My GOAL" and the changes that I need to have in place to achieve my vision. I brought my vision to life and put in place workable solutions, time tables, look at possible barriers and how to overcome them and to keep focused on the outcome.

I looked at Personal Transitions which will run in tandem with the Business Transition (My Goal) to make sure learning and development is taking place on all levels simultaneously. This will give us all the motivation, desire and strength in depth to achieve and move forward as a joined up team whilst all the time nurturing talent and development.

Here we make the transition from our current position to where the business needs them to be. This is done on a personal level and a group level, establishing concrete personal goals and business goals. We take a very structured guide to achieve the outcomes, which also double up as a continuous personal development plan as well as a business plan.

We bring parts 1 & 2 together creating our new understandings and learning's, combined with powerful transition plans to achieve your goal. We gain commitment, a clear focus and motivation to align the individuals and teams for the journey ahead.

Getting started

I now have my vision, outcome, values and a development process; I can take the first steps on the road to success. Firstly let me understand where I am now and how I got to be here. After I know this, I can then put my plan of action together to where I want to be.

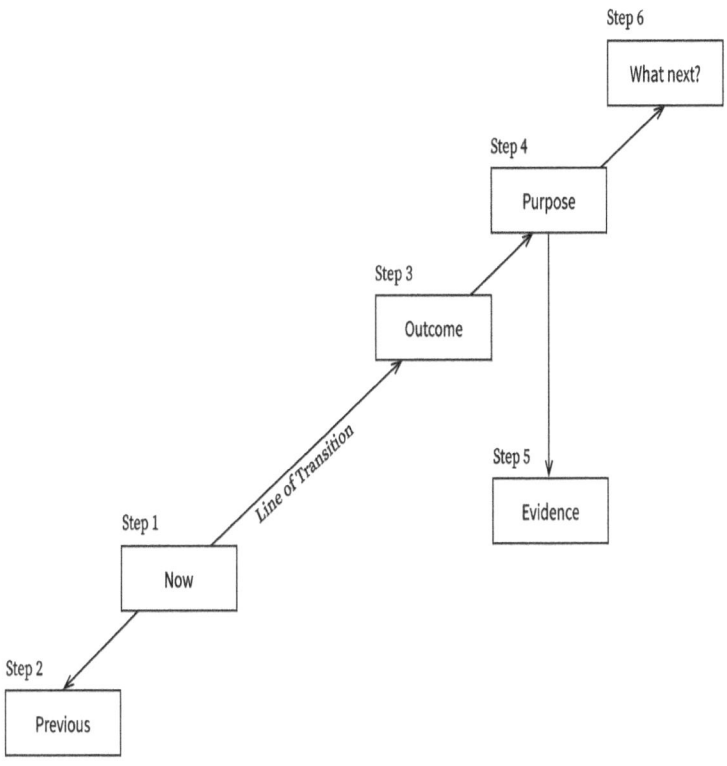

The Steps of Your Journey to Your Vision

- **Step 1-** I fully understand exactly where I am now as a business. This has to be brutally open, factual and honest with no excuses. I need to play with a full deck of cards, otherwise I have tripped over at the very first hurdle and trust is automatically broken.
- **Step 2-** I will need to back track and explore how I got here, what I have done or more importantly; not done to find myself in the present situation. Again honesty and playing with a full deck of cards is a must for clarity and to execute a fully operational outcome and help not to make the same mistakes, or fall into the same traps as before.
- **Step 3-** I am now adding to the journey *my vision*, the single most important reason why I am in business. My vision/goal. What it is I will achieve, what it will do for me, the business now I have achieved it and the teams who are joining me on this journey
- **Step 4-** I will now need to think carefully as to the reason as to why, the exact reason and purpose for choosing the vision I have chosen.
- **Step 5 –** How will I know when I have achieved it? What will be different? What would have changed? How are the teams different? How is the business different? How will the changes be measured and compared? How will I identify what has been achieved.
- **Step 6 –** What next? Now I have achieved my outcome, is that it or do I keep moving forward? Where does the business go from here, what is my next vision?

All steps are interlinked and important; one cannot be completed without the other. Step 2, is crucial for motivating my team. Unfortunately, some people do not believe in themselves from past experiences. By backtracking where I came from, to where I am now, demonstrates that I can achieve, as I have moved from one place to another. To make that change, something must have been achieved to do this and highlights the fact that this has taken place.

Step 5 also plays a significant role here; understanding what will be different when I have achieved my goal, how will I know when I have achieved it. This is vital to make sure the vision I am setting out on, is the one I want and have thought it through correctly. It explores the outcomes in detail and will stop as so often happens when people achieve their goal, it wasn't what they expected or realised the impact it is having on them or another part of the business.

Step 3. How I achieved my vision, fully immersing myself, vividly visualising and experiencing achieving my goal. The feelings, imagines and sounds, completely, running through my entire body. Standing on step 3, looking at step 2, still fully immersed in my achievement, I start putting in the plan I did to achieve this, the individual steps I took along the way, the process I used to move from step 2 to step 3. As mentioned earlier, working backwards from my vision, tells my mind that I have already achieved it, I just need to put the detail on the transition line-my plan.

I also use this same model and process for individual appraisals/ performance reviews, as it genuinely about the individual and their own personal development plan. They have control over their future; they decide how they wish to develop, it is my role to help them achieve it.

Another way I use this multi-purpose model is for planning; I use it as an individual plan, a team planner and for my vision planner. It is a simple tool; however I have found it to be a vital part of my business. HR now use it when conducting interviews, same process and it keeps the interview professional, on track and lets the interview fully engage with the potential employee.

Working backwards from achieving my goal, removes that temptation to give up. If my goals or outcomes are stated in the positive and being able to vividly visualise them, I can immerse myself into believing that I have already achieved them, my chances of succeeding are far greater as my unconscious mind is trained to succeed and continues in this new positive, can do attitude, have done, way of thinking. It becomes my new normal way of thinking.

The old saying "**seeing is believing"** rings true for people, however the successful people reverse that saying, stand it on its head and rephrase it to become" **If I believe it I will see it"**

They believe anything is possible, they believe fully in themselves, their vision and the teams they work with. Success for all will override comfort and the easy options, to deliver on the vision and ultimate rewards.

Throughout "Taking the first Step", I have broken the processes down, and simplified them as much as possible. In some cases, you may feel a little further investigation, reading or research is needed to gain a fuller understanding of each part. However, reading it undisturbed and letting your mind become curious, it will allow the learning's to be understood, so you can then apply them to your business.

Using the process, Step 4-Personality traits will only be effective once I have mastered and applied Steps 3,2,1. Step 3- Communication will only be effective once I have mastered steps 1.2. and so on.

Using the different steps as stand-alone modules will only give you limited results with no real purpose as to why I am doing it. They are all interlinked, feeding in to each other. It is a chain reaction; all the links must be there and in the correct order to be effective to achieve my vision

The Cultural Triangle

The Service Level Indicator

The Equilateral Triangle is the strongest shape known to humans; it is balanced, all sides and angles are equal, interlocking, forming a continuous solid structure from wherever force is applied. I need to build my business on the same principle so it can stand the test of time. Each side of the triangle works interdependently to form this structure, yet forms as one to give it the strength that can withstand any amounts of pressure.

Although each side works interdependently with the other two sides, they are all of equal importance to its strength. If too much emphasis is place on one side, this will then weaken the structure, which will in turn cause the triangle to become unstable and possible collapse.

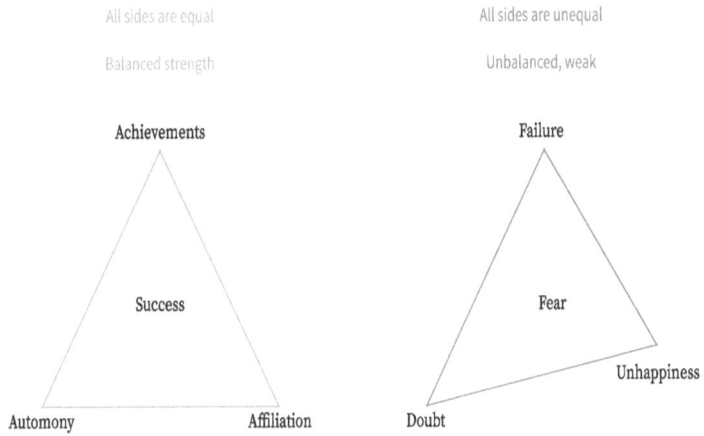

With all three sides of the triangle being equal, achievement is in the hands of us all to achieve my vision, not just me or a few of the team. This removes the pressure to perform were people can freeze or not perform at their optimum because of fear. Fear of making mistakes, fear of failure, and fear of self-doubt. Removing this pressure or fear, allows people to perform freely allowing the creative juices and imaginations to flow with the weight of stress off their shoulders.

The need for <u>Achievement</u> is the need to achieve something better for self and others than it has been and be recognised for those achievements.

The need for <u>Autonomy</u> is the need to have influence, to be responsible and accountable for self and others. Being able to express myself

The need for <u>Affiliation</u> is the need to truly feel accepted, understood and appreciated

We all have needs and I have a duty as an employer to get my teams needs met. This hits the spot of motivation for the staff on a personal level, a collective level and for me personally. With a highly motivated team, performance increases, output increases and collective excellence bonds the business together.

Autonomy

Autonomy gives you power, it can be used in two different ways; a healthy way or a not so healthy way. Expressed through two choices; Power reflects the influencing of others, defeating an opponent or competitor, winning an argument, or attaining a position of greater authority. People with low need for power may lack the assertiveness and self-confidence necessary to organise and direct group activities effectively; they have no choices or very limited choices at their disposal.

A high need for power may be expressed as "personalised power" People with high-personalised power may have little inhibition or self-control, and they exercise power impulsively. The actions of these people have tendencies to be rude, and collecting symbols of power, big offices, desks, fancy cars, titles and egos to match. When they give advice or support, it is with strategic intent to further bolster their own status. They demand loyalty to their leadership rather than to the organisation. When the leader leaves the organisation there is likely disorder and breakdown of team morale and direction.

Socialised power need is most often associated with effective leadership and relationships. These people direct their power in socially positive ways that benefit others and the organisation rather than only contributing to their own status and gain. They seek power because it is through power that tasks are accomplished. They are more hesitant to use power in a manipulative manner, are less narcissistic and defensive, accumulate fewer material possessions or symbols of power or status, have a longer-range perspective, and are more willing to receive consultation and advice. They realise that power must be distributed and shared, and that everyone must have a sense of influence over their own jobs.

Effective people empower others who use that power to enact and further their own vision for others and the organisation.

Achievement

Achievement is reflected in attaining challenging goals, setting new records, successful completion of difficult tasks, and doing something not done before. High need achievers prefer a job in which success depends on freedom to deliver, effort and ability rather than on chance and factors beyond their control. They prefer tasks that enable them to exercise their skills and initiation in problem solving. They want frequent and specific feedback about performance so they can enjoy the experience of making progress toward objectives. If achievement is dominant driving force and the pressure is on to succeed, these people may try to achieve objectives alone rather than through team development, or become paralysed through fear. In either way the targets to be achieved will not be reached and all the efforts will become fruitless. It actually becomes counterproductive.

Affiliation

Affiliation is about establishing or restoring close and friendly relationships, joining groups, participating in pleasant social activities, and enjoying shared activities with colleagues, family or friends. It reflects behaviours toward others that are cooperative, supportive, and friendly and which value belonging and conformity to the group. They obtain great satisfaction from being liked and accepted by others, and prefer to work with others who prefer group harmony and cohesion. A person low in affiliation tends to be a loner who is uncomfortable socialising with others except for a few close friends or family. They may lack motivation or energy to maintain high levels in group achievements, relationships, and building close personal relations with peers and subordinates so necessary for the work place and having a sense of belonging.

Those with strong affiliation needs are reluctant to let external influences interfere with harmonious relationships. Moderate affiliation needs are related to effective working harmony, since strong needs often lead to avoidance of unpopular decisions, permitting exceptions to rules, and showing favouritism to friends.

This often leads to people feeling confused about rules, playing to the manager's likes, and becoming anxious about what might happen next.

Cultural Triangle Service Level

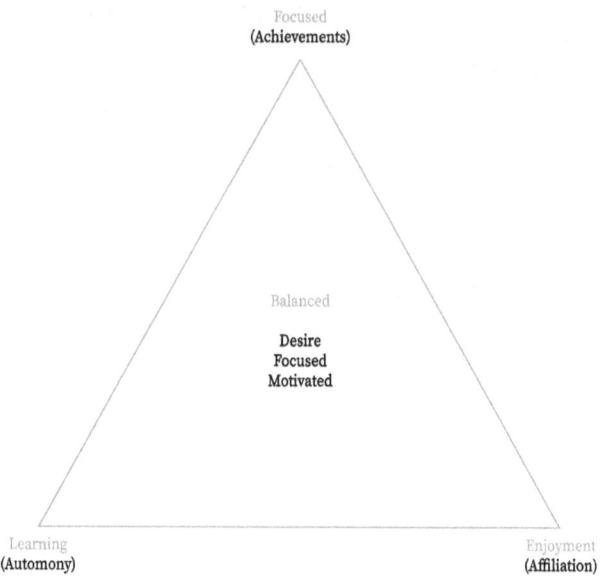

Three rules of performing

1. *Achievement-* Reaching your full potential, Believing in self and others
2. *Autonomy* -Having the choice to learn and develop, not enforced robotic learning.
3. *Affiliation*-Being Understood, appreciated, respected and treated with dignity

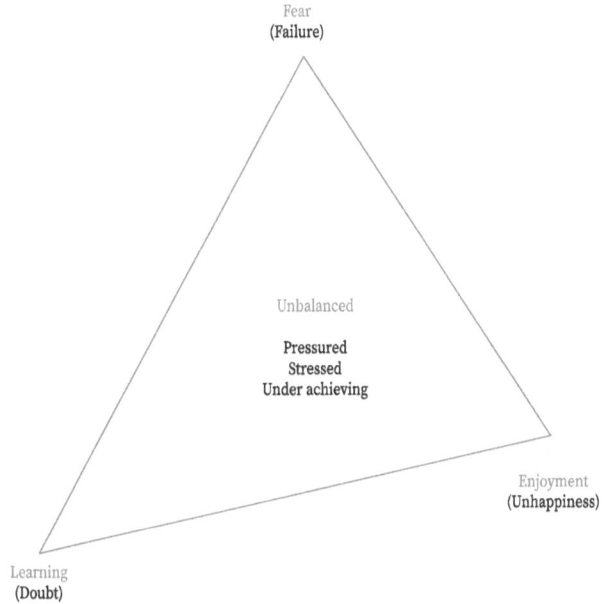

Three rules for under performing

1. *Fear*: Unable to perform, pressure to achieve targets
2. *Doubt*: in the company, own ability, values, self-esteem, and purpose.
3. *Unhappiness*: Not belonging, under achieving, underappreciated, no choices

Demotivated workforce

I believe and found out the hard way that there are four key factors in the workplace that causes resistance and de-motivation; getting the job done seems impossible and just causes never ending battles with employees. The de-motivating factors I believe are fear, unhappiness, doubt and stress-They are all interrelated and whether you have one up and running or all four, the consequences are still the same, people being ineffective.

Fear- this could take in a number of factors
- Not finishing deadlines
- Missing budgets and turnover
- Loss of self-esteem (fear of failure/success)

Unhappiness-
- Not feeling appreciated
- All work no play
- One step forward three back
- Increased pressure and work load
- Lack of support

Doubt-
- Start doubting one's own ability because of increased workload
- Doubting others ability and integrity (Feeling of being used)
- Doubting why you are doing what you are doing
- Doubting even positives and looking at the negatives all the time

Stress-
- Increasing the pressure on yourself
- Unnecessary burden of workload
- Being a perfectionist
- Staying at effect rather than moving to cause.

The way I tried to eliminate these de-motivators is to create a climate where Choice, Belonging and Control for each and every one of us has (Cultural Triangle).

Failing to remove these de-motivators only led to the teams and me being completely ineffective and under performing at a level that was at a dangerous point to where the business stagnated and became a very toxic environment to be in.

These I found were fairly easy to remove, by collectively creating set values and behaviours to demonstrate those values in work. These values then became self-monitoring, raising standards and mutual respect to each and every one of us. Again this falls into the self-awareness, cause & effect and blind spots category, the damage it causes a business, through negativity, employee relations and staff turnover is frightening. Yes, it took me a while to repair the damage caused over the years, it was a long process undoing poor or ineffective systems and delegating more. It was less painful than continuing on the path of self-destruction and sleepless nights.

Once in place, it was like someone had flicked a switch and the workplace was unrecognisable to what it had been. Was I dreaming or wishful thinking-no, it was real, it was happening and I sat wondered why on earth had this not been done before. Sometimes I guess I could not see the wood for the trees, being in the middle, fire fighting and dictating. I do sit and wonder about some of the really good people who had left because of the four de-motivators that I had allowed and encouraged to exist in the work place.

My new Understandings

These were my new understandings, what were yours and how did you apply them?

The strength of the team is the leader and the strength of the leader is the team. That strength comes from a common purpose, great work ethic, agreed values and behaviours, which in turn establishes a work culture conducive to achieve-together. Competition for market share and a bigger slice of the financial pie is difficult.

Other companies competing for the same slice of market share, standing in front of me, are not the enemy, they are the competition. The enemy is behind me, right inside my business in the form of, untrained staff, disengaged teams, not sharing the values and having a very clear understanding of my vision.

The need to have everyone motivated and engaged is crucial; it will make or break me. It didn't matter how good my vision was, or how motivated I was, I needed each team member on board to deliver for me.

It took me time, just like a great painter/decorator or builder; it is all about the preparation or foundations. I understand fully now, building a foundation of my vision of sand is very unstable and will shift or collapse when conditions work against me. Spending extra time in this area and preparing the staff for the journey ahead, is time well spend. It saved me time, money and headaches further along on route to success.

I fully understand now that for any behavioural change to take place in me or my teams, a change in perspective needed to happen.

Step 3: Getting my Vision Understood

The third step is all about communication. Communication needs to be accurate, positive, alive and delivered in a method than is clearly understood. I discovered peoples learning styles and the way they interpret communication and make sense of the message being delivered. Understanding peoples learning styles helps getting my message and others on how we understand the world. 7% of any message is the actual content, 38% is the tone (delivery) 55% is the body language

Each of us has a different way we learn, processing of information and delivering of information. There is no right or wrong or better or worse, it is just the way we are hard wired and perceive the world. Getting information across that is understood, accurate and meaningful first time is a skill that has to be fine-tuned to each individual or teams. It is the same message; however that message needs to be presented in a way that it meets those learning styles of employees in the business.

Communicating accurately saves time, money, and energy it keeps people engaged and also they understand clearly what is expected of them and others. We have all come across situations where we have repeated ourselves constantly and whatever the message is, it doesn't get acted on correctly or not at all. Many times this isn't down to the staff member being lazy, incompetent or a negative hard nose individual, most times they just haven't clearly understood the message coming across to them. It is more about the spoken word; tone comes into play, body language and their particular learning styles.

We cannot, not communicate, we communicate all the time, and it's not about the message, it is how we deliver that message. It is vital we do not leave information, my vision to chance, I need to make sure it is clearly understood for effectiveness

As a leader, I can only operate in a positive state of mind. My intentions have to be right to ensure that the message is received and understood, also acted upon.

If my message is negative, condescending or trying to pull the wool over their eyes, it will be seen straight through and the communication is then broken and closed down

It becomes extremely difficult to communicate after this as trust is in a very short supply and the teams star looking for hidden agendas.

Communication Intentions

Whatever my intention is from the outset towards a personal relationship, a meeting, tuition or a business transaction, this will determine the outcome, the quality of communication and the speed in which that communication is received and understood.

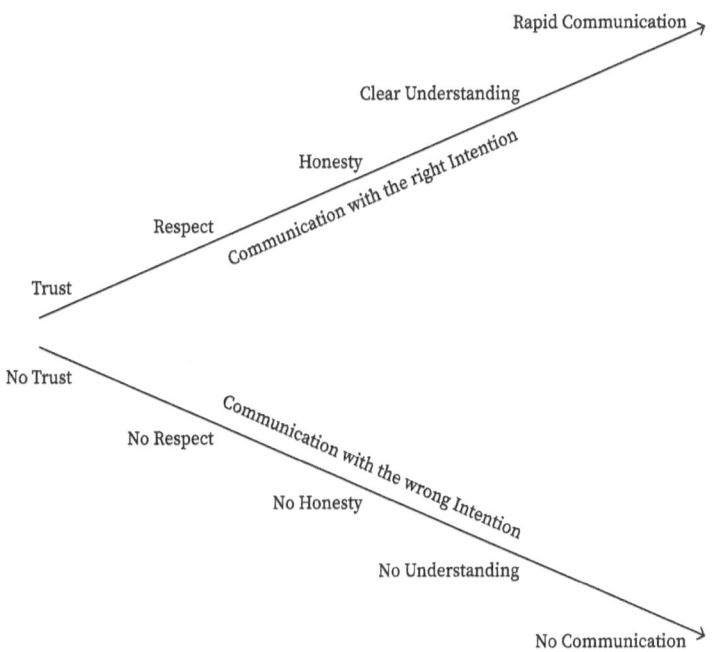

Every human being has a preferred or default representational style, how we interpret information, how we process information in our surroundings and give it meaning. These styles are not better or worse; right or wrong; it is just how an individual makes sense of the world. The main representational styles fall into three categories, Visual. Auditory and kinaesthetic (includes Olfactory and Gustatory). We all constantly use the different styles; however, we have a preferred or a default style, especially at times of stress or in a pressurised situation. Understanding which a person's preferred style is, builds rapport, making communication easier to interpret and to make sense of the message. The message I delivered had to be done using one of those styles to gain greater meaning and impact. It allows the person to fully engage in the conversation and process the data in a way that they understand and are comfortable with. I started to use visual language for the visual representation people when communicating with them, whether that was written or orally. They needed to be shown things, to see what was happening, where we were going, they needed to be focused. Likewise for the auditory group, they need the interaction to ask questions, they needed to discuss as to being shown, they wanted to be told how it should be done, an exchange of opinions through dialogue. The kinaesthetic was more about how they felt about the vision, they needed to feel it, be comfortable with the process. This is not to say, non-visuals do not do auditory or kinaesthetic, we use all three, and however understanding which person is which, gets to the heart of the matter far quicker. It builds rapport, the key to positive human interaction by engaging communication.

Understanding these representational styles gave me a light bulb moment, one of those of course it is moments. I looked at human relationships and my working environment; what I observed and concluded was:

In the workplace I noticed this played a key part in communication for relationships on all levels. As managers, male or female, we predominantly revert to a visual style of operating, watching what is going on, keeping an eye on things; this came across as big brothers watching us all the time. The teams however were predominantly in kinaesthetic mode. They did not believe the managers understand them, listen to them or know how they are feeling and what it was like for them on a daily basis. When I think about it, the visual representation is extremely dominant, I look at the figures, observe the teams behaviour, view the processes, keep any eye on what's happening, watch the finances; all to do with looking and seeing. I had to get the managers and myself to snap out of this, by using the kinaesthetic representation, empathy; putting ourselves in their shoes to motivate them and bring them on-board. This is the only way I and the managers could really connect with the teams; yes we use all the representation modalities, we just need to be mindful of which one we are operating in. This conscious decision to use a representational style for the right situation and person unlocked their potential and broke down any resistance to change. This is one of the key factors in the difference of being a manager or a leader; a manger tends to stay in visual mode and a leader uses all representational modalities that make the individual response more effective. It is about being self-aware and understanding the people and the teams that they make up.

This was a very powerful insight for me and one which is now a way of life; it pays untold benefits as now both me and the teams understand and are fully understood.

Trying to force our own representational system to engage with a different representational system completely dilutes the message. As a leader, I need to be flexible enough, smart enough to interact with others, so I can communicate effectively. When I am trying to communicate, I don't start by trying to pull others into my shoes. Instead, I stand in their shoes and ask myself,

- Do I understand what this person is saying?
- Do I understand fully this person's situation?
- Am I offering choices or alternatives that will help this person move forward?
- Does this person understand that I understand them?

Traditionally in the education system, the prominent styles are visual and auditory. Commonly we hear teachers saying, be quiet (Auditory) and look at the board (visual) and so on. Now that's ok for these styles, what about the kinaesthetic, their learning styles are not being addressed. They have to work twice as hard to understand the lesson as they are delivered in visual and auditory styles.

The same for my meetings, I have to address all styles to get the message across and understood.

With the amount of information we receive and deliver, the human mind has to do something to help deal with all this data. Running alongside these learning styles; with all this information around, which I now realise, is bombarding me constantly, millions of bits of information per second. That amount of information hitting me cannot all be dealt with by my conscious mind, I would be overwhelmed and unable to cope, so I need to filter out the bits that are important to me and discard the rest.

When I think about it, if this is happening to me, it has to be happening to the others; they are filtering out the information that I am sending them, just taking bits they need and discarding or ignoring the rest of it. This I found was not intentional behaviour; it was a natural way of humans dealing with vast amounts of information as a coping mechanism, an unconscious response to survive the information tsunami.

The upside of this unconscious response is coping, the down side is they could be deleting vital bits of my message and only working or dealing with the parts they have filtered and then filling in the gaps of the message with their own interpretations. Wow, that is scary, and I do understand now, why things are not getting done, done badly and the results I am getting are much hit and miss.

I now never assume that my message is understood just because I have said it in a way that is meaningful to me, as it could be completely foreign and misinterpreted to the receiver of the message, who will naturally make meaning of it in a way that is meaningful to them. As a leader, I am responsible for the message being understood. As airline pilots do, if the Captain gives a message or instruction, the co-pilot repeats the message or instruction so there is absolutely no misunderstanding, as this could potentially be a life or death.

The same is done with the pilots and the control towers, nothing is left to chance, and the message is repeated back for accuracy and understanding. The aviation industry, the military, emergency services all use the phonetic alphabet; scientifically designed, so that a critical combination of letters are most likely to be pronounced and understood by people exchanging voice messages. Strict adherence to the prescribed spelling of words is required in order to avoid the problems or confusion.

Now my business may not be a life or death situation; however, it is a situation that means success or failure. I cannot over emphasise the importance of clear communication and its understanding that can only be done by having a process in place where it is checked and a high level of importance attached to it.

In order for me to cope with information, I will do three things; I will either.
- Delete the information
- Distort the information
- Generalise the information

These as previously mentioned are coping mechanisms, which we as humans rely on to survived for the information tsunami that continually heads are way. The flip side is, we are missing out on vital bits of information that could be of vital importance to us.

I now know that I need to be aware of that the message is understood and that it is interpreted as it is meant to be. That works both ways, from me to the team and the team to me.

Communication can make or break a business, it can render me as a leader who could be ineffective and my teams paralysed with fear of making mistakes and heading off on a project in completely the wrong direction.

This I found was crucial to achieving my vision. Having understood the impact of Deletion, Distortion and Generalisation, I had to make sure that I was very specific in sending my message and also when listening. I had to get right down into the detail by asking question such as.

- "How specifically do you mean it will not work"

- "What exactly are you comparing it to"

- "Who exactly said what and to whom"

- "Does this mean you cannot do it or you won't do it?

- "How specifically will that work"

This is a key area where information can go astray and slow the whole process down of achieving my vision. Spending a little more time drilling down on the specifics of the message; saved me and the team's vast amount of time in the long run and helped removing the frustration that can occur from misinterpreting a message.

Deletion- This is where we leave part of the message out. - We are deleting large chunks of the message.

When we listen, we unconsciously delete much of the message being delivered and retain only bits of the information. This saves us time as we would be unable to process each and every word being spoken. When we speak, we reduce on all the details that we could share. This helps us to become more efficient as it gives us a filtering system of large amounts of information so we do not become overwhelmed. When we delete information, we then have to fill in the gaps in any conversation so we assume the rest of the message. If you told someone you purchased a new suit and don't tell them what colour it is, or where you purchased it from, then they would begin to guess more information and fill in the gaps missing on the information. This creates a problem when we constantly delete information, it becomes a habit, and we constantly misinterpret and misunderstand what exactly the message is. We become mind readers and second guess the message.

Distortion- This is where we fit the information to suit our own experiences. – We fit the information to our own reality and perspective of the world.

Distorting the information makes us not always represent the truth; it only gives us meaning to our own version of the truth. We match it against our own previous experiences, and give it our own meaning depending on how we interpret or view those experiences-We make it up to fit in with our own reality as we make our own connections to the information. If we continually learn to distort with everything, it will eventually create a belief system within us that would hinder our rational thought process. That belief system will only make us understand the situation from our own perspective and will not take into consideration the others persons view, beliefs or perspective from their understanding.

Generalisation- This is where we standardise a meaning of something- A chair; it has four legs, a back, a seat and arms- by standardising we miss out vital details of the information or message. The chair could swivel, go up or down, rock forwards and backwards. When we think of a chair, which we learned the word chair as a child, so we would be able to recognise and name it the next time we saw one.

If you had a poor experience with a certain company you would probably generalise that all its outlets were poor. Having strong generalisations can cause us to become quite judgemental as we put people into boxes or categories without giving them or the situation the necessary appreciation that is needed to fully understand it.

The art of communication for me is; listening. I have been taught how to write a letter, how to speak at a meeting, how to delegate and how to present a project. Not once in my entire life, even during my education at school, has anybody ever taught me the art of listening-and it is an art.

Really listening to others is the power behind great communication. It uncovers what people are really trying to say, what their values and beliefs are and why they are important to them, I can begin to understand them and empathise with their points of view. From this position of empathy, I can respond and motivate others in a way that is important to them and mutually beneficial to all.

I also find it important to challenge my own beliefs, why I believe in something and why is my opinion different from others perspectives-what do they know or see that I am not, what is different for them to the same situation as we are both in. What is on the flip side of the coin?

I started to challenge others and me, politely with curiosity, by exploring different opinions and views. This opens up more choices and options without watering down my vision, being flexible in my approach to achieve my vision collectively.

Not really listening to others and surrounding me with yes men, I believe is very dangerous as it makes my beliefs extremely rigid and inflexible and not allowing my vision to have life breathed into it, it hardens my stance on issues or suggestions that there is only one way to do it, and that's my way. "Do as your told and don't question it"

Listening intently, questioning respectively will make communication flow more easily and openly, otherwise it is like pushing water uphill.

Make your teams and me become curious, feed our curiosity and expand our minds to what is possible and what can be achieved if we can all be an integral part of the vision and aligned in our thoughts.

Different levels of Listening

Do I listen with one or two ears?
How do I really listen?
Do I even listen?
What level do I listen on?

6. **Understanding – Gains maximum Results**

5. **Listening to Understand**

4. **Active Listening**

3. **Selective listening**

2. **Passive Listening**

1. **Hearing**

I think about it in this way, the strongest person in the room is not the one who speaks the most or who is the loudest. They are only telling you what they already know; and don't listen to discover anything new. The strongest person is the one who listen's the most; they learn new information and observe the people around them to understand and gain new knowledge and perspectives.

Gaining Rapport Through Communication

The content of what I wish to say is only a very small part of the total message. If my tone or body language does not match the content, my message will be missed and not acted upon. If my teams are in doubt, they will pick up the message and interpret it from my behaviour and how I am saying it rather than the content itself; which I need to get across.

I needed to relate to others in a way which created trust and understanding with my teams collectively and on an individual basis. This I did through rapport by creating an honest and open dialogue were all felt comfortable and the freedom to get their own point of view across without being judged or fear of recrimination from others. Rapport gives all of us and especially me being the leader, the capability to see each person's view point and putting me and the teams on the same wavelength; here we could appreciate everyone's understandings and feelings. Rapport creates great respect, fairness and appreciates the other person, whether I agreed with what they were saying or not.

- 7% of the message is what we Actually Say- the message itself, the content

- 38% of the message is the Tone we use- How we are actually saying it

- 55% of the message is the Body Language we use- Our behaviour whilst saying it

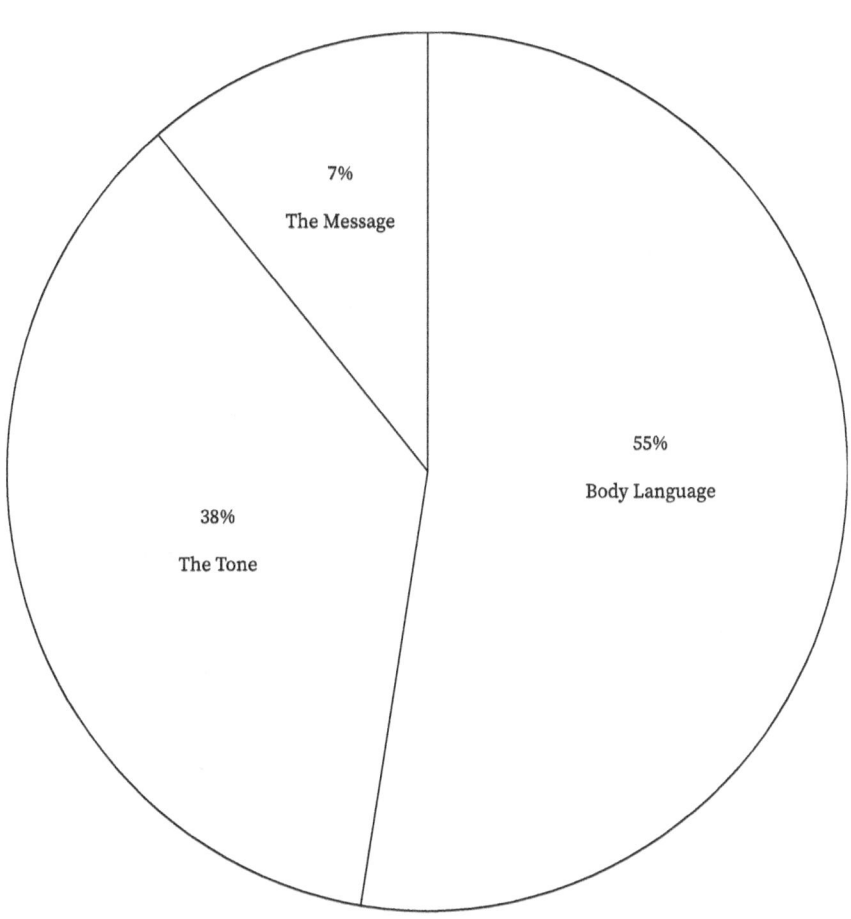

My New Understandings

These were my new understandings, what were yours and how did you apply them?

The engine room of my business comes from the senior and middle managers; they are the heartbeat of my vision. They keep the communication channels open with information flowing freely both ways, up and down. It is crucial that this information, my vision is interpreted correctly so vital parts are not missed or misinterpreted. Great communication keeps everyone in the business fully informed and engaged; they feel part of my vision, no matter how big or small that contribution is.

Getting my vision understood needed clear and accurate communication, listening acutely and having an awareness of what was happening around me. Listening to others is essential to achieving my vision. If I didn't and just kept continually talking, then I did not learn anything new, I was only repeating what I already knew. For someone to make a change in their beliefs on an issue there has to be a change in perception for them

Being in a position where I can influence others, I needed to be very aware of how my actions and words impacted on them. Everything I do has a consequence, so I needed to understand those consequences.

Part 4: Personality Traits

The fourth step brought it all together and I got a great understanding of where people's views in the business are and how I will bring about change, understanding healthy and unhealthy responses and how to interact with particular views. These are the human hot buttons that make people tick and react in ways that I can now understand. I have learned how to get the best out of them and what is needed to develop them to the levels I need them to be at to deliver on my vision.

I looked at the structure in the work place through values, personality and perceived life views of the work force. This clearly demonstrates how conflict is caused and avoided, what their thought process and views on life are, what is important to them and what is not important. I looked at what their reaction to change is, the healthy and unhealthy responses and how to deal with each situation.

Bringing everything together from part 1,2,3,4, blending it to maximise my understanding of behaviour in the work place and how to use those understandings to deliver collective excellence consistently. Being motivational, inspiring and focusing on achievement, reduces painstaking, time on time consuming HR issues that can be avoided in the first place. Managers will have a profound impact on others and self by creating a positive future through change rather than by chance, which will ultimately deliver on my vision. I aim to move managers from thinking like a manager and develop them into leaders in my business where the culture is about Affiliation, Achievement and Autonomy

Personalities and Behavioural Traits

Before I could enter the leadership phase, understanding each individual's behavioural traits and how they would respond in a positive situation and react in a negative situation. This was very important, so that I could understand each person's strengths and weaknesses, how each person operated mentally, their thought process and most importantly, what personality type was required to carry out certain tasks. Just as important, is understanding my own trait and how the teams perceive me.

Every work place is filled with the different personality traits, these are neither right or wrong, better or worse than each other, it is just how we are hardwired. These different traits are working constantly throughout the working day, this is how conflict occurs in the workplace, a major source of disruption if not understood and worked with. Choosing the right personality for a particular task was the difference that made the difference. If I needed a tough no nonsense approach to get the job done, I selected a personality type that suited that profile. If it was a detailed administrative role, then someone with an attention to detail, dot the I,s and cross the T,s profile was used. This type of personality traits selection for certain tasks ensured that I had the right person to do the right job that needed doing. This uses everyone's strengths to the maximum effect.

Apart from saving time and effort by having the task completed correctly first time, it also involved every person in the organisation. I made it a priority to understand and used effectively every person's trait to accomplish different tasks, rather than relying on just a few to carry everyone else kicking and screaming to where I needed them to be. I used these traits not only for accomplishing the required tasks, also for team selections, rotas, project managing and new employees joining the business. This allowed me to get the correct balance in the business, harness the huge pool of talent, to gel a dynamic work force capable of achieving great things for me, the business and themselves. In "Taking the First Step", everything is relevant to achieving my vision, this part though for me was the most critical and influential that now all my future plans and visions are based around the personality traits. I really cannot over emphasise the significance and importance of this process, and urge you all to give it the time, understanding and respect that it deserves.

By using the personality traits, this allowed me to keep all the teams involved, engaged and contributing to the vision. They all played a part in the vision and believed that they were being valued as an individual and a leader in their own right. Having every one of the team fully engaged, earned me and them credibility, respect and a true belief in each other to carry out their own individual roles and the support to others to complete theirs. It is like a giant jigsaw, everyone in the business is a piece of that jigsaw and it cannot be completed until everyone has come to the table and placed their part.

This was collective excellence at its peak, utilisation of the complete work force, learning and development on a grand scale by believing in what I had done so far in the process, the development of the teams and a stoic belief in the individuals within the business.

The best way to describe using the personality traits is putting the pegs in the right holes. Square pegs in square holes, round pegs in round holes. It really is that simple, using the correct person for the situation that requires attention.

Understanding people's personality traits, values and views on life has a profound impact on the business and working relationships. It builds trust, honesty, respect and a complete understanding of each individual and lends to an environment which is non-judgemental, where people are free to express themselves because they are understood and understand

Communication becomes free flowing, open and misinterpretation of the message is far less likely to happen when you can understand each other without judgement and a clear expectation of each other's capabilities at that moment in time.

PERSONALITIY TYPES

Nine distinct personality types.
Nine different perspectives on life,
Nine ways of being in the world.

1. **The Reformer. (Perfectionist)**
   Can lead through integrity and reason
   Can be hindered by perfectionism and resentment.

2. **The Helper.**
   Can shine with generosity and healing powers
   Struggles with people pleasing and possessiveness

3. **The Achiever (Performer)**
   Inspiring example of excellence and authenticity
   Blindly pursues success and status

4. **The Individualist**
   Can model creativity and intuitive power
   Held back by moodiness and self-consciousness

5. **The Investigator. (Observer)**
   Demonstrates visionary intellect and inventiveness
   Becomes eccentric and isolated

6. **The Loyalist (Questioner)**
   Exemplify courage and commitment
   Struggles with anxiety and rebelliousness

7. **The Enthusiast (Adventurer)**
   Highly accomplished and spirited
   Waylaid by impulsiveness and impatience's

8. **The Challenger (Asserter)**
   Powerful and magnanimous leader
   Control and intimidation

9. **The Peacemaker**
   Brings people together and heals conflict
   Held back by passivity and stubbornness

UNDERSTANDING PERSONALITIY TRAITS
(approaching each one)

1. The Reformer. (Perfectionist)
They can have a very strong internal reference which makes them good decision makers.

They can be pragmatic and get down to business right away. They don't need too much small talk, since they are objective, exact and want the detail. To be effective they need cold hard facts rather than excitement and enthusiasm be specific, and keep all your promises, and always be on time.

2. The Helper.
They are very people orientated, so before getting down to business, build rapport. Who is telling them what to do is just as important as to what they are doing. They prefer generalities rather than details unless they are really necessary. Show them you care and have their best interests at heart.

3. The Achiever (Performer)
They are image orientated, enthusiastic, intense, hardworking, go-getters and usually good decision makers. Part of their motivation is to prove to themselves and others they can achieve. Anything that can help them show off their status or success as well as achieving more will gain their interests. They love being the first kid on the block. Be direct, positive, enthusiastic that focuses on what they want or need to achieve

4. The Individualist
They need to be made to feel wanted, unique and special. If they are telling you a story, never try to better them. Envy is their primary sin and you will go back and forth until they eventually withdraw. Be sensitive and non-judgemental when dealing with them. Avoid crude, harsh or loud behaviour as this will make them withdrawn.

5. The Investigator. (Observer)
They like very detailed information and not too much big picture. They will make up their own minds based on how the information and facts are presented to them. Too much detail and they can become overwhelmed and confused and will get lost in trying to make a decision. If too much information, they will, need help piecing the facts together to come to a decision, otherwise they won't come to one and go around in circles. They need gentle guidance as opposed to direct influence.

6. The Loyalist (Questioner)
They are generally filled with doubt; decisions are generally tough for them. Don't give them too many choices and certainly don't shift gears on them. Having a stable, grounded presence can help. Being wishy-washy or constantly changing your recommendations as well as discussing anything negative will only fuel their anxiety. Never pressure them into making a decision; this will do more harm than good. Since they go back and forth in their heads about making the correct decision, be aware that they may congruently say "YES" today while, without any obvious reason, tomorrow that yes will become a "NO"

7. The Enthusiast (Adventurer)
They are very aggressive, outgoing people. Lots of energy, enthusiasm and love attention. Therefore match their energy enthusiasm by being upbeat and positive. Make them the focus of your attention and talk in terms of how the new idea/product will help them. They will go accept what you are saying if they are swept up in excitement; dull and boring will not hold their attention for long no matter how important the information is.

8. The Challenger (Asserter)

They like to be in control and have a strong internal reference. This makes them excellent decision makers and need to feel that they have decided for themselves. Try to avoid telling them what they can and can't do and place the decision in their hands, give them choices or options. Tell them straight and don't sugar coat the information as this will insult them and this could turn to anger. If you have a strong recommendation, hold your ground and don't suck up, they respect strength and loathe weakness. Match their intensity, if they are mad; get mad with them-NOT AT THEM.

9. The Peacemaker

They are passive, like the familiar, and are very feelings orientated. Typically have a more hands on approach (kinaesthetic) as opposed to visual. Speak slower to build trust, spend more time as they will trust you more. Be calmer and less over excited and enthusiastic as this will come across as aggressive. Their primary sin is laziness so will not be on top of things like most others. They are not dynamic and need constant gentle reminders to complete tasks instead of direct pressure. Pressure has the opposite affect and slows them down rather than speeding them up. Decision making is difficult for them since they have trouble prioritising.

WHICH PERSONALITY TYPE ARE YOU??

The Reformer

The Helper

The Achiever

The Individualist

The Investigator

The Loyalist

The Enthusiast

The Challenger

The Peacemaker

Different Personality Traits
My new understandings

Having gone through the process successfully on a number of occasions now, I have come to the conclusion that, any new knowledge, training or development is not only about what I have learned, it is about what I have understood, and how it is applied from those learning's, Understanding the new learning's allows me to remember the new found knowledge and also to apply it in many different ways that it maybe was not intended for.

This kept my mind curious and open to new ideas and suggestions, remaining flexible in my approach to achieving my vision.

These were my new understanding, what were yours and how did you apply them?

Getting the best out of any person or situation is the key driver in the business. Managers in modern business spend 40%-50% of their time on a daily basis dealing with employment issues. That adds up to a very expensive waste of time, talent and potential loss of business. This is Shrinkage to the business that can never be recovered or sustainable for periods of time. A manager is there to drive the business and my vision forward, by engaging teams and focusing on the end goal rather than unnecessary HR issues. Having upfront knowledge of how people think, how they will respond will give me and my managers the edge and to remain focused on what we were employed to do.

Understanding behaviours and personalities, keeps my eye on the ball and having the business continually moving forward, as opposed to stop, start because of issues that do not have to be issues.

Part 5: Managers v Leaders
"The strength of the Team is the Leader; the strength of the Leader is the Team"

Before my goal started free flowing into action, the final piece of the jigsaw was to develop all the team members into leaders and move them away from a managers thought process. Managers are fine for looking after systems and people who can't look after themselves, I needed far greater passion and desire than that, I needed leaders who would stand up and be counted, who would be creative and courageous whilst still showing compassion. I want people who wanted to achieve and not settle for second best.

Now there is not a great deal of difference on paper to differentiate between the two, however in practice the impact of those actions is profound and carry huge consequences.

Everyone in the business operating as a leader, from the lowest to the highest ranking, gives them a real purpose, a sense of belonging and an appreciation that their contribution, in whichever way is important, valued and respected. The simplest of ideas can contribute with the largest impact. People who feel a sense of belonging will bring a continuous flow of ideas from perspectives that others may not see or thought about. A collective workforce is the engine behind my vision, the driving force and energy to succeed, the glue that bonds everyone together and has the strength to keep on pushing forward, even when on occasions defeat stands in the way of the vision.

So what are some of these differences?

Managers	Leaders
Managers focus on systems, they enforce the rules and are rigid in their approach	Leaders understand and develop people, they have the ability to connect to others without effort
Managers will behave according to the rules and guidelines. This is the way it's done, don't deviate away from them	Leaders do the right thing for the right situation, they are flexible, knowledgeable and don't procrastinate
Managers don't like change or cannot implement it effectively in the fear of failure or resistance.	Leaders adapt, searching for new ways, ideas and always moving to improve
Managers try to rule with threats and an iron fist, it's my way or the highway	Leaders Inspire others to be the best they can be, share ideas and encourage new thinking
Managers focus on the detail and themselves, they are in it only for them	Leaders are consistent, have bigger ambitions and visions for all who follow
Managers stagnate and operate out of instruction	Leaders are always pushing the boundaries, looking for new horizons and challenges

The functions of both are similar, however the execution of the functions are the complete opposites. The leader's impact is far greater in strength, influence and inspiration. It carries a very positive approach to life and to work with a focus on achievement, belonging and self-control, leaders are creative, compassionate, and courageous with a belief in themselves and others.

Moving all individuals irrespective of their role in the business to a leader's way of thinking creates a dynamic environment. Every person feels they are contributing to the vision, and being part of something unique, rewarding and having a purpose for what they are doing. Great leadership is not a skill, it is an attitude; driven by the individuals values and beliefs to be the best they can be.

"A leader who does not listen to their people, will only end up surrounding themselves with people who have nothing to say"

Good habits of Leadership

- **Self- Control-** If you cannot control yourself, you cannot lead others. Self- control sets a strong example which followers will emulate

- **Decisive** If you waver in your decisions it shows you are not sure of yourself, you cannot lead successfully

- **Attitude-** To be pro-active, Positive and encourage staff to bring out the best in them in order to follow

- **Courage-** To inspire and motivate the desire to achieve (not to dominate). Being a smaller part of the bigger thing with self- confidence and courage

- **Responsibility-** To accept responsibility for the mistakes and short comings of the followers, dust off themselves and go again

- **Empathy-** To Empathise and have understanding with the team, to make decisions with the full picture to a positive outcome

- **Definitive-** To deliver faultless plans of leadership that creates a positive and inspiring learning environment (continually)

Bad Habits of Leadership

- **Inconsistent-** Unable to organise and master details consistently. A leader is never too busy to do anything of them in their capacity of a leader

- **Fear-** Leading by force and not by strength of character and consent. Fear as a leader someone may take their role by teaching others

- **Imagination-** Without imagination a leader is unable to perform in emergencies and creating plans to lead effectively

- **Aggressions-** Followers do not respect any form of intemperance, it destroys any long lasting relationships and trust

- **Disloyalty-** Lack of loyalty is one of the major causes of failure in life. The disloyal leader cannot maintain their position with colleagues at any level

- **Authority-** A true leader has no need to advertise the fact except through their actions and demonstrates that they know the job at hand

- **Selfishness-** A leader who claims all the glory for the work of his colleagues will is sure to be met with resentment. A true leader claims none of the glory and is happy to see the glory go to his followers and knows they will work harder for recognition than for money alone.

Monitoring Effectiveness Rather Than Results For Success

I work in a results driven business and the results need to be measured to ensure the business is on track to achieving its targets and my vision. The results tell me whether I am successful or not.

I can measure these in two ways;

- I can Manage results
- I can Coaching/Lead Effectiveness

When I manage the results, this way is the big stick approach to achieve targets. I discovered it had a short term impact; however it reverted back to its original position, as staff did not buy into the vision and became demotivated and looked for excuses as to why it will not work and undermine the business and my vision whenever they could. Managing results, does not give me a true reflection on the business and how we are performing; it misses out on key and vital ingredients that underpin my business operations. It does not give me the full picture as to how we achieved the results.

Coaching/Leading effectiveness- this placed the emphasis of achieving firmly at the employees doorstep for the roles they are employed to do. I exchange with them a salary for their time, effectiveness and value to my business. So to ensure I was getting a healthy return on my investment, I needed to coach/lead them through the results process by making them effective, accountable and responsible by contributing fully to the business in order to make my vision a success. I could not allow people to be carried, not pulling their weight and putting in their fair share of the work load. This is overlooked when purely focused on results.

Measuring effectiveness looks not only at the figures (£), it also looks at the individuals and what they are contributing to that success. It allows me as a leader to be fully aware of the individual members who make up my teams and what their contribution is, their effectiveness and do they give me value for money. It all leads to the results in the business and its success.

Below is a performance sheet I used to really get the best out of my staff. I could get to grips with each person's contribution and how effective they are to me, their colleagues and my vision. Any below par performances I addressed immediately to correct them, I could not afford to have unhealthy seeds being planted in the business. Once they take root, they can germinate very quickly and the disruption to the business and my vision could be disastrous. I did not allow myself comfort over the issue and turn a blind eye to issues that arose; I dealt with them appropriately and quickly when they arose.

I found using the performance/effectiveness sheet removed those issues as people became more effective and self-motivated to achieve, it really made them accountable, in a positive way. It became self-policing in the end.

The first column is the criteria for effectiveness, the further three columns has the questions above it which they need to answer for each question in the criteria.

The questions may look repetitive asking them 3 times, however it is rephrasing it in different ways to stop them giving excuses, nonsense answers and trying to pull the wool over my eyes as a leader. It plants the responsibility and accountability firmly at their feet; it encouraged self-reflection and self-correction. Using it correctly and in a positive manner, yielded me fantastic results to achieving my vision.

The criteria I used for monitoring effectiveness in beyond the first step are my own and applied them with great passion and focus to keep me on track to achieving my vision. You may wish to draw up your own criteria.

Monitoring Performance/ Effectiveness

Criteria	1. What value do you bring to the business? (What are you doing?)	2. I am investing in you, what return on that investment is the business getting? (How are you applying it?)	3. How effective are you in the business? Score 0-5
Learning and Development			
Accountability			
Responsibility			
Responsive			
Pro-active			
Focused on the bigger picture			
Achieving			
Autonomy			
Affiliated			
Moving towards Goals			
Values driven			
Remain at cause			
Aware of self and others			
Motivated			

Needless to say, if a person is not being effective and contributing fully, then I had to have that conversation immediately to address the issue and mutually agree a plan of action to correct the behaviour and bring them up to the standards that I required. I drew up a simple effectiveness contract that matched the KPIs we had set in the business. This contract ran alongside the normal employment contract, with appraisals, and effectiveness monitoring.

By doing this, I found it to be very constructive, getting the best out of people and giving myself and the teams a more balanced and informed view when it came to decision making. It was a great motivating factor for individual performances and every one could see exactly where they were, what changes need to be made to achieve the desired outcome. It also made sure that we all pulled our weight and left nowhere for people to hide or become free loaders.

Sharing the Workload of Effectiveness

Balanced Relationship

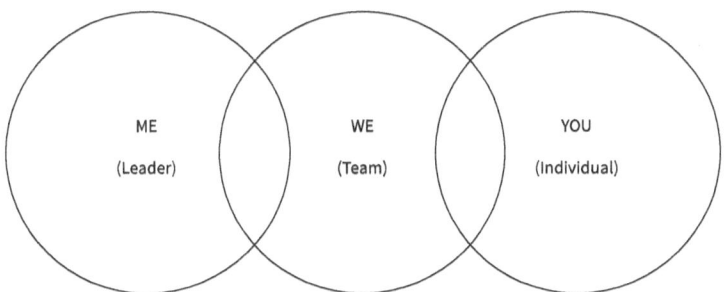

Having a balanced working relationship ensures everyone in my business is involved and contributing their fair share of effort to the vision. This is collective excellence, every person being responsible, accountable and being part of something greater.

This is the ideal I needed to work towards to have maximum effectiveness in my business.

Not sharing the Workload -Ineffectiveness

An unbalanced Relationship

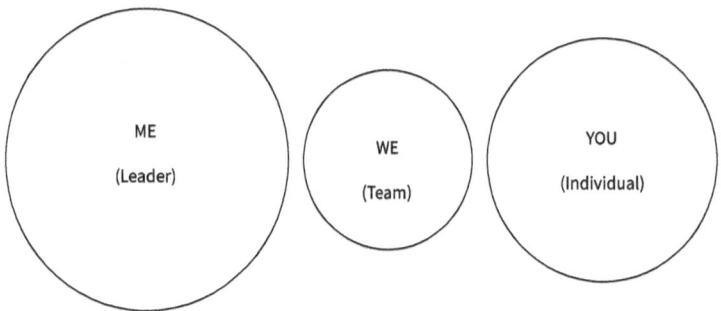

Having an unbalanced working relationship has the reverse affect. Not everyone is engaged or bought in to my vision .People are working as individuals and not joined up as a team. People are not taking responsibility, being accountable and would rather stand on the side-lines than getting involved and contributing their fair share. This is when I heard the comments "It's not my Job"; as soon as I heard these words, or similar, I knew I had employees and not a team. Negative staff will always find problems to solutions. This was a wakeup call "Change needed to happen"

Influencing Behaviour Through Understanding

Key components of our personality are what we call deep filters. These filters are deeply embedded and along with our values will determine how we respond to situations. They will also relate to our preferences when dealing with information.

Understanding these filters for me was essential to bring about the change in behaviours of my teams that I desired, also how I communicated with them. Having this knowledge gave a great awareness of how to communicate effectively with my teams and to influence them in developing themselves and belief in my vision.

To use the deep filters effectively, I deployed them in a few areas of my business.

- When I was interviewing for a particular role within my business
- Selling my vision to the team
- Developing team spirit with having the correct mix of personality styles
- Enhancing all the relationships in the business through awareness of ourselves and others
- Motivating the teams
- Any communication between ourselves

The list is not exhaustive; however you can see the importance it has for me in key roles in my business.

There are around 20 of these filters that operate in each and every one of us, every second of the day. This is why I needed to understand them to make me and the teams most effective. I narrowed the range of filters down for me to 5, which I find the most important at any given time.

The filters sit either side of a spectrum and somewhere along that spectrum we all sit. Knowing where about on that spectrum people sit with their different filters, allows me to influence them and to make sure all my communication with them is effective. Understanding where somebody sits on the spectrum is understood from listening carefully to the words people use, the patterns and how their sentences are structured; it reveals an enormous amount of information about their make-up. Most of the time they are unaware of how they structure their words, by listening very carefully it will let me understand them. As a leader, I needed to operate on their point on the spectrum, not mine when dealing with each individual and through positive communication and influence, try over time to move them along the spectrum to a leader's perspective. Not doing this, we both had conflicting views on things; we need to be on the same hymn sheet so to speak.

A very important observation which helps my decision making process is; if a person has their filters sitting on the right hand side of the spectrum, I found they did not make good leaders or managers. They were on a level of supervisor at best; that is not to say they could not change and progress, however it needed the awareness of their filters for change to be brought about successfully.

I needed to understand my own filters also to see how I responded to situations; and to situations that arose. Communicating using these filters, with any individual or team, I found even makes generic training or information become very personal and of importance.

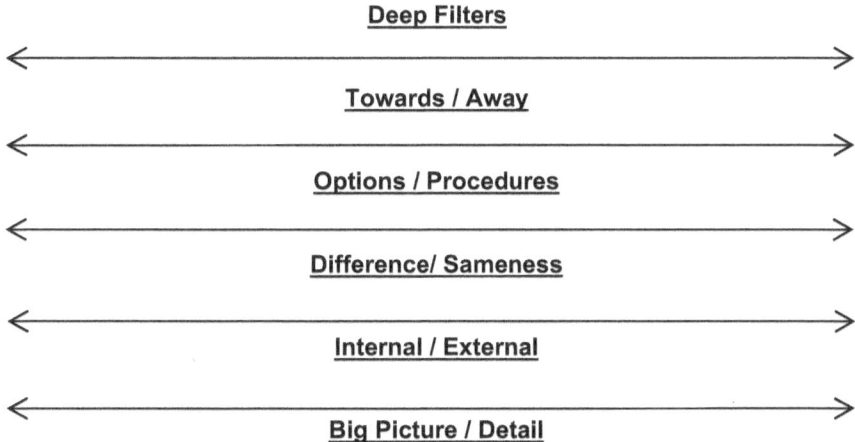

Pinpointing where each staff member was sitting on the spectrum of the different filters gave me a great understanding as to where their focus was and how their thought process was engaging them.

Using the criteria from the examples helped me and them find out where they were and what sort of approached should be used to motivate them and to get their buy in.

This information is vital when training, meetings and wanting to get the teams focused by using language that they understand clearly.

Filter	Key Traits	Mention and Influencing
Toward	Stays focused on goals and targets.	What they would win, achieve, to have, get. Give targets.
Away	Notices what is wrong, Problems to be avoided.	Situations to avoid, things they don't want to happen
Options	Seeks new and different ways to do things, willing to bend the rules. Dislike of procedures.	Be flexible-offer several options and choices.
Procedures	Likes to follow established procedures.	Offer/suggest the right way to do something. Steps to take.
Difference	Likes frequent and significant changes, notices the differences.	Change and point out how things have changed /different
Sameness	Likes things to stay the same, dislikes change, and notices commonalities.	Keep things the same, point out how the situation is similar to what they know.
Internal	Sets their own standards, knows what is right from their own judgements.	Use phrase as " you may want to consider" "what do you think" "only you can decide"
External	Needs feedback and input from others.	What others think and say.
Big Picture	Thinks in overview and conceptually. Dislikes detail.	Provide overviews. Use words like "essentially, overall, in summary"
Detail	Likes and needs the detail.	Details, specific, precise, exactly.

Conclusion

Principles for Successful Goals

1. **Know exactly my outcome-** If I can clearly define **my** outcome appropriately, then the outcome will be more achievable. I do not start anything without knowing the outcome/goal I want in advance.

2. **Self-awareness-** I have an acute awareness of what is going on in **my** work/life as you proceed to **my** outcome. What new things are happening in others?

3. **Have behavioural flexibility- I am** willing to do whatever it takes to achieve success. Here is **my** key to success- with enough rapport and enough behavioural flexibility; I can always achieve **my** outcomes/goals.

4. **Build and maintain rapport-** I create a climate of Trust, Respect, Honesty, Happiness and Unity. I build a culture that is positive and nurturing through strength of **my** leadership.

5. **Operate only from a Physiology and Psychology of Excellence-** I only operate from a totally positive resourceful state. I only do things that empower you and others.

6. **Take action-** Without action and taking the first step, there are no results for **my** goal.

Summary

What have I learned, how have things changed for me since following the process in Taking the First Step and applying it? How has that change impacted on me, my vision and my business?

My journey from the dark depths of despair, working aimlessly without focus or direction, lost in a quagmire of negativity, HR issues and stress, to going beyond the first step and seeing my vision in action has taken me on a path of personal discovery and change. I have a greater understanding of me and of others; a key ingredient in human relationships either in the workplace or in a social environment. I have now developed as a person and a strong leader, a leader who the teams now want to follow for greater success.

I have learned this through understanding my blind spots, self-awareness, values and the impact that these have on people. Every action, every word, every behaviour, every thought has a consequence on others; and being a leader, I need to be fully aware of those consequences; I need them to work for me not against me.

I now understand that values are emotional attachments of people, the key drivers behind a person's behaviours. It allows me to understand what is important to me and others. It gave me the opportunity to have set values agreed by us all in the business with behaviours that demonstrate the values. This gave me collective excellence, a culture of mutual respect, positivity and a focus on achieving my vision, pooling together in order to make sometimes the impossible possible. Every new vision I have, we create a new set of values that sit in harmony; the alignment of the vision and values is the dynamics of achieving, it will overcome any barriers, hurdles on the journey to success.

How I communicated was a great lesson in life for me; I needed to listen more to understand to truly get behind what was being said and also what wasn't being said.

Total listening and careful questioning unlocked the real meaning of the message, so I could respond to it appropriately. It also builds a relationship of trust, respect and a belief that I really did care about my teams and not just paying lip service to their input. If we talk about our thoughts, I know this is governed by our beliefs, if we talk about our feelings, then this is governed by our values; I needed to tread very carefully when challenging these, as I will now start to challenge their core existence, a powder keg ready to go off if not done skilfully. I realised this was a challenge, however it was a challenge that needed to be done and not left; otherwise positive change would not be brought about and my vision would remain gathering dust on the shelf.

Understanding the individuals and the personality traits allowed me to make best use of the person for a particular task. I used people's strengths and skills that were needed at the time, this engaged all the team, and everyone had a part to play. By using the right skill set, it also kept the culture of positivity as people did not find themselves struggling to accomplish the task and hiding any embarrassment.

Putting all my new learning's together, I keep reminding myself that, it is not just what I have learned, it is really about what I have understood from those learning's and how I am going to apply them. If I don't apply them and share those understandings, taking that first step will become harder and harder, over time and my vision will remain a far-fetched dream that was never brought to fruition. I now clearly understand before taking the first step, where I am to where I want to be, and changing from what to what.

The only thing holding me back from taking the first step was me. My own limitations, the tiny voices in my head, I was listening too much to the people who doubted me, taking their opinions more seriously that my vision. Once I had taken that first step, the shackles came off, and although the journey at times was tough, I never stopped believing, not to prove others wrong ,or to prove me right- this made sure I was doing it for the right reason-"for me and my goal"

I likened my business to a game of snooker

Imagine the business as a game of snooker; it is a very tactical game and a battle of skills, experience and outwitting your opponent to score more points than them by potting the balls into the pockets in the correct sequence. This time though, the game, it's in the workplace and your balls are the staff. Potting the balls takes different techniques depending on where they are situated on the table, another ball blocking it, a slight nudge, a full on power drive or to gently manoeuvre the ball around the table until there is a clear shot on the pocket you want it to be in.

Only when all things are aligned, the cue ball, the ball you wish to pot, and the pocket you wish to put it in; using the right amount of force, will you be successful in achieving your goal. Too much force or miscuing, the ball will either bounce right back out of the pocket or you will slice it off on an angle sideways and completely miss what you are trying to achieve, and leave you with another or different issue.

The same can apply for when dealing with your staff, the consequences are the same, except now they are in human relationship terms with a lot more at stake. Only when the business, its values, its goals, its business plan and its people are aligned, will it become successful. Your role is to get the best out of each team member by using an individual approach to get the best out of them, rather than a scatter gun approach and hoping for the best.

If you do not do this, just like in snooker, the balls will be all over the table, giving away your control and advantage to the opponent.

Each pocket on the table represents a different learning or development, for each staff member, for their personal development and improvement to the business.

The pockets could be:

(1)Motivation, (2) Effectiveness, (3) Autonomy, (4) Accountability, (5) Values/Beliefs, (6) Achievements

- You as a leader become the Cue ball; however the cue ball can only strike another ball by being in a positive frame of mind.

- If you use a negative, word, behaviour or action, It becomes a missed shot; the team then have they're turn; a chance to push back and move around the table repositioning themselves, creating further issues and changing the situation of your goals. It constantly becomes a different picture

- You need all the balls on the table to be cleared before moving to the next stage of staff development and achieving my goal.

- Every time a ball is potted, a new skill is learned and development takes place.

You have to continually pot the balls in the different pockets to develop the staff and move towards your goal. In order to do this and understand each team member's needs, you need self-awareness, properly laid out plans, communication and being the leader they expect you to be,

Looking at the snooker table and the layout of the balls on it, it is not straight forward. As a leader (cue ball) I have to operate all around the table, in very different situations, with different skill sets and knowledge on how to put the balls into individual pockets without damaging them or putting each ball into the same one. Like the balls on the table, every staff member has different skill levels, knowledge, and ability. Sometimes a ball may be blocked or not in the line of sight of a pocket; in this case I need all the skill sets available to me to carefully move the ball around the table without touching another ball or putting it in the wrong pocket. The only tool I have is to move is–"A positive frame of mind" otherwise, in the words of the game, I'm snookered.

Using a negative frame of mind only achieves narrowing down my options and creates tension, frustration and hampers my progression- the teams push back and try to reposition themselves and each other to give them the advantage and we never get beyond the first step.

As a great leader, I have to adapt my style and approach, staying in a positive frame of mind only; applying it to each individual as one size does not fit all. The way to achieve this is knowledge, desire, communication and having great people skills. Putting all this together allows me to manoeuvre the balls around the table seamlessly, with a plan and focus on what it is you are trying to achieve. Anything else will leave you confused and frustrated. Leadership, learning and development is a process, not an event, "I have to own the process" Only by using all the newfound knowledge that has been made available to me from the book, I can achieve my vision by applying the different skill sets to the relevant situation.

Benefits from only operating in a positive frame of mind

- How will the game play out for me if I can only be in a positive frame of mind?
- What would be different for me only using positive and nurturing techniques?
- What would be the impact on my business? What would be different in it?
- How would the behaviour of the staff change? What would be different for them?
- Would I get my vision in action and achieved quicker?
- What is the positive impact on Achieving, Affiliation and Autonomy? Learning and Development?
- What would be the financial impact to the business in staff retention and progression?
- This is why I need to go "beyond the first step" and make my vision come true.
- I need to own the process.

I honestly believe that the only way to operate my business is through being positive, pro-active and values driven. Continually being in a positive frame of mind, builds trust, respect, integrity and honesty; which I find essential in any work place, not just mine. The alternative is to approach everything from a negative frame of mind; the impact is the total opposite and extremely detrimental to my vision, the business and the people who work within it. The financial impact of negativity on the business through poor leadership has the potential to destroy it or at best leave it in a quagmire of disillusionment, unproductive and a daily battle to achieve the minimum of tasks. Operating from a negative frame of mind, demonstrates that you have lost control and do not own the process; your focus is in the wrong direction.

Yes I had to change, at first it was difficult and strange, kit did feel uncomfortable as I had to keep myself in check and not slip back into old habits. Was this pain worth it?
Absolutely; like with any situation, hindsight is a great thing and only wish I had brought about this change earlier on in my career; it is never too late to change.

Practicing daily my new found skills is the only viable option to achieving my vision and being successful; not only in business, also in human interaction and relationships; "Collective Excellence"

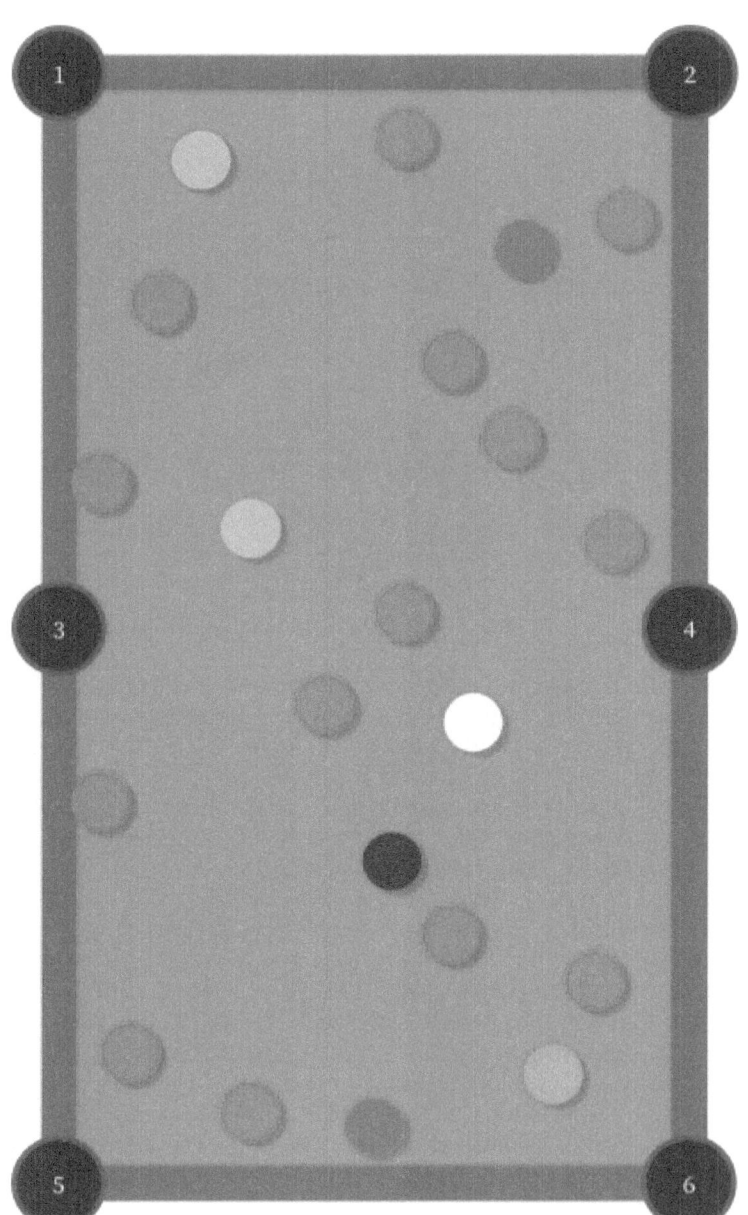

Author

Passionate About Inspiring Others

I have learned the hard way in life and business, which has given me very valuable lessons about people, values and dignity that I will never forget. Although I don't have University degrees or the privileges of a private education, I do employ people who do have them and I surround myself with people who are positive, visionary and curious who share the same passion to achieve for themselves and others.

I had to find another way to make my business work for me and for me to success in the business world. I had to use the one skill I had, people skills. How to motivate people to be the best they can be, how to truly understand people and how to work with them to achieve. Yes, I had to polish up on those skills, learn some new ones and change the way I thought and behaved- it was a change that I will never regret and one I continuously repeat when I am out coaching and developing in others business's. I believe it is fundamental in business for success. The days of poor management, dictatorships and toxic work places are over and doomed to fail. Teams want to know from their leaders now and in the future, how much they care about them before how much they know.

I have worked with a wide variety of situations and people over the years, which has given me a broad outlook on life. Nothing gives me more pleasure than achieving goals, coaching and seeing people flourish, and making a positive change to their lives. This is achieved by strong leadership, listening, hands on approach coaching and being proactive to achieve results. Everything I do is done with Creativity, Compassion and Courage.

I am qualified and accredited in Coaching, Psychotherapy, Hypnotherapy and an INLPTA Master Practitioner. I have blended these Psychological disciplines with management practices and people development skills, ensuring that business is getting the best out of their team and making them professional, efficient, with a positive can do attitude at all times.

I have operated my own business, employing 54 staff of varying levels of education and skill levels. This has given me the knowledge to treat every person as an individual and work to their strengths, irrespective of backgrounds, in a non-judgemental way, giving them the best opportunity to be the best they can be.

I have achieved Gold standard in Investors In People, by running a fully inclusive operation, investing time and effort in staff development, harnessing those results and skills, then delivering on what we promised. "The Vision" by utilising peoples personality traits.

Working overseas for 10 years further educated and developed me with hands on training, dealing with different cultures, people, problems, language barriers, sometimes in very difficult situations, this has helped me become flexible, have great self-awareness and remaining calm under pressure to remain focused.

As a volunteer, I worked as a Counsellor for the Yorkshire Cancer Centre which operated out of St. Michael's Hospice in Harrogate (outpatients). This was extremely rewarding working with patients, survivors and their families who care for them. By using the same blend of disciplines, in a very complex environment to bring about comfort, hope and a possible brighter future.

For further information on how my business can help your business, please visit or email me on;

www.leadingforsuccess.wix.com/fwsc

www.facebook.com/leadingforsuccess

leadingforsuccess@hotmail.com

Other books-

"Boredom in the Workplace" (Motivations Silent Destroyer)

Resources
Resource Guide
© 2000, Albert J, Valentino Personality Selling; Vantage Point Publishing, PO BOX 267 Islen NJ 08830-0267

©2002-2011 NLP Master Practitioner Manual Dr Susi Strang Associates Saltburn-by-the Sea, North Yorkshire UK TS12 2EF

© 1988 Tad James & Wyatt woodsmall, Time line therapy and the Basis of Personality, Meta Publications, PO Box 1910 Capitola, CA 95010

© 2010 Jeremy Lazarus, Successful NLP for the results you want, Crimson Publications, Westminster House, Kew Road, Richmond, Surrey UK TW9 2ND

www.ingramcontent.com/pod-product-compliance
Lightning Source LLC
Chambersburg PA
CBHW031443210526
45464CB00005B/2316